Published by Workplay Publishing
Bluffton, Ohio 45817
workplaypublishing.com

ISBN 0-9842122-1-3

Cover design and layout by Alison L. King

PRINTED IN THE UNITED STATES OF AMERICA

QUALITY VICTIM ADVOCACY:
A Field Guide

DAVID L. VOTH, M.A., L.S.W., C.A.

WORKPLAY PUBLISHING

This book is dedicated to the resiliency of crime victims.

Contents

The introduction illustrates how victim-centered advocacy is the link connecting the four movements of victim assistance, victim rights, violence against women, and restorative justice. We do not just aim for quality services, but also for systemic changes and prevention, regardless if an arrest is made. This book is not a guide to the science of individual change or research on intervention techniques. It is about designing, measuring, and duplicating the art of victim advocacy, and our calling to serve victims.

    A. What is victim advocacy?
    B. How does victim advocacy tie the victim field together?
    C. How do we get to a victim advocacy mindset?
    D. How does prevention relate to victim advocacy?
    E. Does victim advocacy have a moral basis?

The four components of quality victim advocacy are: 1. access—services being visible, reachable, acceptable, and available; 2. structure—the right services provided with good governance, partnerships, tools, and staff; 3. process— treatment that is ethical, professional, uniquely provided, and sensitive; and 4. outcomes - meeting victim-directed needs of safety, healing, justice, and restitution. Each quality area can be measured for implementation, effectiveness, and efficiency.

    A. What are the key components of a quality program?
    B. What are we trying to measure?
    C. What are the indicators of a quality organization?
    D. Is efficiency a quality issue?
    E. Chapter summary

Victim advocacy programs exist to help victims improve their lives. Traditional and U.S. Department of Justice measures such as process, expertise, efficiency, and quantity are important and need to continue, but program goals should define success by changes in victims. Victims are our customers, and they deserve to know if we have a plan and record of success in meeting actual needs.

    A. What is an outcome?
    B. Do victims have common outcomes?
    C. Do outcomes fit with the U.S. Dept of Justice Global Challenges?
    D. Does federal funding address performance-based assessments?
    E. What is our anchoring principle?

The classic outcome logic model is like a formula that shows how inputs (resources and parameters), activities (work and effort), and outputs (the sum of your work) are all linked with outcomes (improved victims' lives). Measurable changes in victims' lives are in (ABC KISS) **A**ttitude, **B**ehavior, **C**ondition, **K**nowledge, **I**nsight, **S**tatus, and **S**kill. These changes come in stages of initial, intermediate, and long-term outcomes. Logic models can be adapted to explain the theory of change (design), the outcome achievement plan (a link between work and outcomes), and the activity progression (how to manage).

The victim outcome logic model shows how needs of victims for safety, healing, justice, and restitution (financial recovery) are related to later and earlier needs. To accomplish the initial, intermediate, and long-term needs, victim services are directed to a particular outcome. The logic model is a guide for Victim Advocates to understand which services, and in what sequence, might help victims reach their individual needs. There are influencing factors within each victim, the type of crime, the variations of the systems involved, and in the program design. Your logic model is based on victim-driven needs that you can reasonably influence and you have the resources to attain.

H. What are the primary influencing factors for outcomes?

I. What do you need to know when you are identifying outcomes?

J. Chapter summary

To know if you are reaching your victim outcomes, indicators of progress are needed that can be measured. An indicator must be directly linked to the degree of change in the victim (e.g. skill, status, knowledge), use an appropriate recording form (e.g. amount, percentage, rating), be from a useful source (e.g. program data, family members), and use a method that can extract information from the source (e.g. documents, surveys, interviews). Results reporting should include known variables and limitations of your source, collection process, timeliness, volume, percent of total, and other factors that affect the data reliability. Accurate indicators of outcome attainment increase accountability and focus Victim Advocates' passion on victim outcomes.

A. What is an outcome indicator?

B. What are some criteria for selecting an indicator?

C. What are common outcome data sources?

D. What are common outcome data collection methods?

E. What can outcomes not do?

F. What issues exist in reporting outcomes?

G. How can you make outcome reports more useful?

H. What is my North Star through all this?

I. Chapter summary

Victim outcomes are the guiding light for staff and program culture, including how to recruit and train staff around outcomes. Staff must know outcomes as a server knows the restaurant menu. Outcomes are used as the basis for job descriptions and evaluations, activity manuals, and governance board agendas. Outcomes can be the basis for grant writing, budgets, and personnel expenses, as well as improving services as methods and results are compared with other similar programs. Outcomes are an anchor for strategic planning, public policy, partnership priorities, and mission alignment. Victim outcomes are valuable to the degree to which they are integrated into the fabric of the organization.

A. How has the culture of victim services changed?

B. What are the internal uses of outcomes?

C. Chapter summary

Outcomes define the agency to victims and to the public. Outcomes are the guide for partnerships, marketing services to new victims, and are critical for attracting funding with an integrated, incremental, and long-term strategy for impacting lives. Well-defined outcomes result in a clear image for the public through a logo, mission statement, and publicity, recognizing that outcomes are not a box to fit victims into; rather, they are the open-ended services that fit victim needs.

Outcomes are the basis for educating partners in the art of victim recovery and preventing re-victimization.

      A. Five external uses of outcomes

      B. Chapter summary

The issues of access, structure, process, and outcomes are a map and measure of success for programs and the victims they serve. It is not magic that improves lives, but rather, through the resources, partnerships, and quality designs of victim-oriented services. Our task is to manage for results, using logic models to do so effectively and efficiently. The horror of crime can be replaced with hope if we learn from victims and each other.

      A. How do you know if you are on the right track?

      B. How do you manage a victim-outcome based program?

      C. How can strong management produce successful results?

      D. Concluding Thoughts for this Guide

      E. Humorous application of an outcome logic model

      F. Chapter summary

  1. U.S. Department of Justice Federal Performance-Based Measures (Chapter 2)

  2. Sample Program Logic Models

      a. Washington State Victim Compensation Program Logic Model (Chapter 3)

      b. Center for Disease Control logic model for Rape Education Prevention

  3. W.K. Kellogg Foundation, Logic Model Development Guide templates (Chapter 3)

      How to use a Logic Model Through the Life of Your Program

      a. Program Planning (Clarifying Program Theory)

      b. Program Implementation (Demonstrating Program Progress

      c. Program Evaluation (Evaluation Questions)

      d. Program Evaluation (Evaluation Indicators)

  4. Sample outcome models (Chapter 4)

      a. Safety outcome model with activities

      b. Healing outcome model with activities

      c. Justice outcome model with activities

      d. Restitution outcome model with activities

      e. Victim Ministry outcome model

      f. Victim Impact Panel outcome model

Preface

What is quality in victim services? Is it measurable? Is it a gut instinct? Can you design a program and train staff to produce it? Is quality what you do, how you do it, or what you have in the end? How do you get staff and partners to care about quality? What makes an organization balanced? Can victims' lives be directly and intentionally improved, and if so, how? Is it possible to operate program services with specific goals, or a shelter with rules, and not violate a victim-driven empowerment and strengths-based service model?

The purpose of this field guide is to answer the above questions in order to support victims' recovery in the aftermath of crime It attempts to paint a picture broad enough to be recognizable by most victims and Victim Advocates, and yet specific enough to be practical and useful. It connects the forest and the trees—in other words, a master plan. However, since victims and service providers are all different, the master plan must be a guide without absolute guidelines. It is a learning model. This guide is geared for application, to be dog-eared and not read like a novel.

This is not a research report or an instruction manual on any particular therapy, intervention style, or service to provide. Rather, it is primarily a guide for evaluating and improving victim service organizations. You will learn how to increase the likelihood of impacting lives through designing focused and effective services. You will find ways to apply good management practices to your victim service program. As a Victim Advocate, you are a dedicated professional trying your best to help restore broken lives. You have little time to step back and ask if your work can be done better. This guide will nurture your passion and give you ideas on how to influence your program's culture and services with a person-centered response that makes a positive difference in each victim's life.

In this guide I frequently use the term *victim* instead of *survivor* or *thriver* or other reflection of the fullness of life possible. I ask for grace, as this is not meant to be limiting or offensive to anyone.

Introduction

"It hath been told thee, O man, what is good, and what the LORD doth require of thee: only to do justly, and to love mercy, and to walk humbly with thy God." (Jewish Publication Society Tanakh, 1917)

What is Victim Advocacy?

Victim advocacy is the profession and practice of providing individualized victim-centered support and systemic change for survivors of crime.

The term encompasses a variety of contexts and meanings (Sullivan & Keefe, 1999). Many prosecutor- and system-based programs prefer the more neutral reference of victim assistance or victim/witness assistance. Some in the field view the term "victim" as limiting, stagnant, and backward rather than forward looking. In other words, the crime should not be the identity of the person (e.g. "He is a victim"), but rather be recognized as an experience after which people can find happiness and enjoy a thriving life.

Since language shapes our reality, some programs only refer to their work as serving "survivors" of crime, such as programs that work with victims in later stages of recovery or focusing on present and future personal successes of the survivor. However, being identified as a victim can be a healing and affirming concept for some people. The term validates their innocence, places the culpability for the evil act on the offender where it belongs, and recognizes the reality of crime as a traumatic and life changing event. In any case, once a person is identified as having been the subject of a crime, he or she is by definition a (past) victim and is a survivor of crime. Recognizing these differences, the phrase Victim Advocacy is used as a term of art, referencing the work of serving the needs of those harmed by crime.

Victim advocacy is about meeting victims' needs. It is a paradox to design and provide victim services both comprehensively and individually. If you have a master plan to help victims, then the inclination is to squeeze victims into pre-set service molds. If you address every victim uniquely, you miss the commonalities that wisdom suggests will ease the healing process for others. This will be a recurring incongruity in this guide for implementing and measuring quality programs and victim outcomes.

For many in the victim service field, this emphasis on individual victim needs and outcomes will be a paradigm shift and an inspiring "aha" moment. For some this framework for quality and outcomes will seem a statement of the obvious. They will wonder why it is necessary to explain a process that they intuitively use to maximize victim recovery.

Thousands of Victim Advocates already provide high quality victim services, but as the victim service field becomes established and we desire to replicate excellence, we need a victim-centered plan to guide us. We need to duplicate the ability to provide excellent services that result in improved lives. This model of victim advocacy attempts to integrate the wisdom of victims and service providers in a structure that can make positive and measurable improvements in the lives of victims.

However, without at least two obvious ingredients, adequate funding and partnerships, quality victim services is simply wishful thinking. Funding is the ever-present bottom line of quality services. If the funding is not there, no one is there to serve victims and to create the critical partnerships across victim service, mental health, legal, medical, and other fields to meet victim needs. Narrow thinking and the magnet-like attraction to routines are also constant enemies. Our measure of quality is how services and organizations meet the single goal of helping each crime victim attain their unique needs. We must be vigilant in focusing and checking our outcome-based services to know if they are or are not improving victims' lives (Campbell, 2006; Sims, Yost, & Abbott, 2006). Victims are not peripheral to justice, and victim advocacy includes doing right by each victim.

Knowing your goal and accomplishing it are two different issues. This book is neither a guide of best practices nor a research summary of safety options, trauma care, legal procedures, or financial recovery. It is not about micro managing your program. Rather, this is a guide for victim-centered organizational architecture with applications for implementation. It is about macro managing your vision of meeting victim needs. It is not about the science of individual change, it is about the art of increasing the effectiveness of providers and services to meet victim needs. It defines the important differences between quality efforts and services, victim-owned changes, and customer (victim) satisfaction. It is intended to improve victim service quality in the hope that the adage holds true: "a rising tide floats all boats."

How does Victim Advocacy tie the victim field together?

There are four overlapping clusters of victim service providers in North America: victim assistance, victim rights, men's violence against women, and restorative justice. Some providers view their efforts as exclusive, while in other jurisdictions organizations serve victims in all four areas. Either way, victim advocacy is the practical evaluation guide and broad philosophical framework under which all four areas can find common ground.

For example, some system-based victim assistance program directors understand their goal as being to provide the fastest, easiest, kindest, and surest (keeping the routine working without gaps) opportunities for victims to be informed, present, and heard in the justice system. Those leaders may not recognize or prioritize the reduction in gaps that victims also need for victim-centered, one-stop, and integrated service centers. Likewise, leaders of restorative justice programs may consider the existing justice process and adversarial system to be part of the problem. There is room for debate and maturation as we recognize the value of protecting victim services with funding, and victim rights with federal constitutional protections, while working to change our paradigm of response to crime to include victim, offender, and community. There is room to care about improving victims' access to courthouse justice while also working to end world-wide gender discrimination of lower economic value, cultural and faith restrictions on dress and leadership roles, and objectification. Justice for victims is about values and human rights, not just legal rights.

These divergent emphases should not overwhelm our similarities. Each type and philosophy of victim services is valuable and significant. Each fits into the victim advocacy framework that strives to center our thinking and actions on the needs of victims, individually and corporately, to survive and thrive.

Victim assistance has developed into 10,000 programs in the United States, many providing niche services for victims, such as law enforcement assistance, victim impact statements, death notification, state victim compensation, and counseling. The goal of victim assistance is more than helping the turnstile turn faster and easier for victims with cookie cutter services. Victim advocacy illuminates the goal of victim assistance providers to offer both niche and mass services with the motivating passion that recovery is both personal for every victim and due every victim. Advocacy and outcomes are not about offering victims the services that you have, but in creating a culture of matching needs with services that will change lives. That is our North Star.

The victim rights movement has successfully created empowering laws in state and federal legislation, and in a majority of state constitutions. Victim advocacy expands the concept of individual legal rights to include the right to individualized services, thus including victims for whom legal rights remain distant, for example, victims in unreported crimes and cases in which there is no arrest. One precept that victim rights proponents have promoted is that victim rights, like civil rights, attach both individually and to a class of people. The history of the victim rights movement battling for individual rights synchronizes well with the individuality of victim advocacy. Victims are not just valuable as witnesses to solve crimes or deserving of sympathy as the bearers of evil deeds. Rather, victims' recovery is paramount as they are the primary customers (victim or defendant) of the justice system.

The violence against women movement encompasses a variety of sexual assault, domestic violence, stalking, and other special emphases. The massive number, severity, and repetition of these crimes upon victims require cultural, systemic, and individual responses. The fundamental power and control issues rampant in society are particularly evident in the sexism pervading men's violence against women. Victim advocacy complements and nurtures this feminism with the overarching common mission to address the needs of all victims, one unique victim at a time. Victim advocacy is indebted to the pioneering work of rape crisis and domestic violence leaders across the nation. Their work has made it common sense to know that each victim has unique circumstances and needs, which may or may not involve any dealings with the justice system. Their mantras of *safety first* and *empowerment* for victims are secure in victim advocacy. The advantage of the victim advocacy worldview is that partners can use outcome goals and language to integrate advocacy across the service gaps without relinquishing their values and histories. We are all in this boat together.

Restorative justice provides the truth that solving the problem of crime is personal, and important to four key stakeholders: victims, offender, communities, and the justice system (Gabbay, 2005; Zehr & Achilles, 1999). These advocates correctly apply the human-centered harm model to victims. Victim advocacy takes this orientation further by prioritizing the need to fund, implement, and individualize victim services and rights. Adoption of victim-driven advocacy services helps deepen restorative justice concepts (Frederick & Lizdas, 2003). For example, one restorative justice service promoted for victims is the opportunity to participate in a meeting with their offenders. This service, victim offender dialogue (also called mediation or reconciliation meeting), is often used by proponents as a prime illustration of the practical application of the restorative justice philosophy. The stories of victims benefitting from this service abound, yet it is a seldom requested or needed service by victims in their recovery process. Victims' need for safety, healing, justice, and financial stability rarely requires a one-on-one meeting with their offender outside the normal court proceedings. Dialogue with offenders involving victims of long-term abuse in which the power and control differential is established can be particularly harmful to victims. Victim advocacy deepens the applications of the restorative justice vision and increases the meaningful role of victims in restorative justice services. Without (victim) equality, there is no (restorative) justice, since "justice isn't served until crime victims are" (U.S. National Crime Victims Rights Week theme, 2005), regardless of whether an offender is identified or an arrest is made. The concept that crime involves broken lives and not just broken laws is a core principle of both restorative justice and victim advocacy.

Victim advocacy links these movements. *Victim assistance* providers are the front door to the police station, courthouse, and probation/parole office for millions of victims. *Victim rights advocates*, though fewest in number, include both the conservative law and order adherents and the liberal civil rights loyalists speaking on behalf of the human and legal rights of victims. The (mostly) heroines calling for men and women to stand *against gender-based violence* continue to endure society's schizophrenic response of horror to sexual crimes while it often has a muted voice against the cultural acceptance of pornography and the epidemic levels of men's violence against women. *Restorative justice proponents* articulate both the personal and systemic problems of crime, striving to integrate theories and applications of recovery and accountability. They are all correct, yet incomplete without victim advocacy. Victim advocacy is our common culture.

How do we get to a victim advocacy mindset?

The best measure of success in responding to crime victims is one that evaluates services and organizations by their impact on all victims' lives in the jurisdiction. Continuing success requires fighting complacency and not allowing creative ideas to dry up. It involves a constant drive for excellence, motivated by a persistent apprehension that we are not keeping up with victims' needs.

Whether survivor or professional, you will need to build the plane as you fly it. Being an expert Victim Advocate is complex. The best advocates usually know little about the influencing factors surrounding the victim and their support system (U.S. Department of Justice, 2003). With compassion, wisdom, planning, funding, skill training, and a laser focus on individual victim recovery, an expert Victim Advocate is an artist years in the making. Life will go on while you "do justly." This journey has a map of outcome guideposts to point survivors and professionals toward a landscape of hope and recovery.

How does prevention relate to Victim Advocacy?

The highest priority for victims is to avoid crime in the first place. However, we cannot eliminate hospital emergency rooms in order to focus on preventive health, and similarly, victim response programs are critical for helping with victim trauma. Additionally, victim advocacy can interrupt crimes, often with police and medical interventions, such as domestic violence, stalking, and child sexual abuse. One of the hills ahead of us in extending the concept of victim outcomes is the challenge of helping victims avoid being re-victimized ("Focusing Police," 1997). Research indicates that one significant predictor of future victimization is past victimization. For example, the risk of new assaults in previously assaulted women was increased more than fourfold, *over and above* the effects of age, race, education, and substance use. Having to remain in violent neighborhoods or being continually accessible to perpetrators (e.g. due to financial hardship, domestic violence, child abuse) increases the risk of victimization (Acierno & Kilpatrick, 2003; Lamm Weisel, 2005; Tjaden & Thoennes, 2006).

Preventing crime and re-victimization is a common sense notion in the vein of fixing a troubling crack in a dam, rather than simply waiting downriver and pulling survivors out of the water. Wisdom is necessary to empower victims while avoiding victim blaming (i.e. offenders are culpable whatever victim risk reduction research exists), statistical presumptions, and prescriptive interventions. However, acting to prevent re-victimization is better than not doing anything at all; the sin of omission can be as wrong as the sin of commission when lives are at stake.

Advocacy involves a large worldview of victims' needs (List-Warrilow, Menard, 2007). It includes confronting the systemic societal and justice system cultures that often mistreats victims. Sexism, racism, and other "isms" that devalue people can be subtle and yet critical in preventing victimization. In other words, the healing ointment of victim services may mask societal inequities and paradigms that allow crimes against certain peoples. We cannot be satisfied to plant individual seeds of hope when harvesting systemic justice is required. Words of hope are never wrong, but paragraphs to the powerful are also needed.

Does victim advocacy have a moral basis?

Helping victims is ultimately a spiritual task. Each person is a spiritual being with a meaning in life. Religions around the world have stories and parables to illustrate the need to be kind to others and to the less fortunate. Islamic teachings in the Qur'an remind followers to treat men and women with kindness and justice, as do many teachings of the Prophet Muhammad (Yusuf, 1999). A teaching exemplifying this from the Buddhist faith is by the Dalai Lama and is entitled "Compassion: A Religion for All" (Buddha's Village, 2004). The Christian faith has the story of Jesus Christ explaining who our proverbial neighbors are, with the story of a crime victim left to die by the side of a road being helped by the Good Samaritan (Barker, Burdick, Stek, Wessel, & Youngblood, 1995). Jesus ended the story by urging his listeners to do likewise (Barker et al., 1995).

We need to answer the question, "How can we best 'do likewise'?" Victim advocacy is a response to that call. Reaching our best requires wisdom, the kind gathered from careful listening to victims, research, and insightful experience. We must constantly be stretching toward the ideal victim advocacy. Being merciful and being a good neighbor are at the core of victim advocacy. Every major religion teaches compassion. Whatever your religious faith, helping victims is a calling from God (Manis Findley, 2004). Let us remember the words of the late Archbishop Oscar Romero, a Catholic Priest from El Salvador (Romero, justpeace.org, 9-9-09):

It helps now and then to step back and take the long view.

The Kingdom is not only beyond our efforts: It is even beyond our vision.

We accomplish in our lifetime

only a tiny fraction of the magnificent enterprise that is God's work.

Nothing we can do is complete, which is another way of saying

that the kingdom always lies beyond us.

No statement says all that could be said.

No prayer fully expresses our faith.

No confession brings perfection, no pastoral visit brings wholeness.

No program accomplishes the entire mission.

No set of goals and objectives includes everything.

This is what we are about:

We plant seeds that one day will grow.

We water seeds already planted, knowing that they hold future promise.

We lay foundations that will need further development.

We provide yeast that produces effects far beyond our capacity.

We cannot do everything, and there is a sense of liberation in realizing that.

This enables us to do something, and to do it very well.

It may be incomplete, but it is a beginning, a step along the way,

an opportunity for grace to enter and do the rest.

We may never see the end results, but that is the difference between the

master builder

and the worker. We are workers, not master builders:

We are prophets of a future not our own.

Introduction Summary

Victim advocacy is the victim-centered and results-oriented model of victim services. It is based upon, enhances, and links the movements of victim assistance, victim rights, violence against women, and restorative justice. Victim advocacy involves immediate response, cultural and systemic change, and prevention of victimization for victims - regardless if an arrest has been or ever will be made. This guide is not about the science of individual change, or the research results of particular victim intervention techniques. It is about designing, measuring, and duplicating the art of victim advocacy already demonstrated by many professionals and programs. Being merciful and serving victims is a moral and Godly calling by all religious standards.

Chapter 1

Designing Victim-Centered Quality

Organizations are like humans: their parts are interconnected, and their quality is not accidental.

What are the key components of a quality program?

John and Jane Doe face the barrel of a gun while being robbed of not only their possessions, but also their feelings of neighborhood and trust. Who can help them? Will someone be able to answer their specific questions and meet their particular needs? Will they be treated with respect and dignity? Will it do any good in the end?

The ultimate test of quality in victim services is the experience of each victim rather than how many victims were helped and how many services a program provided. The hub of the quality wheel to which all services must align is the victim, our customer. Of course, the best design is of no use to a service provider who is not personally committed to excellence. Our guiding principal is that each victim deserves victim-centered and victim-driven services.

Success boils down to a strategy of addressing four components (Donebedian, 1998):

Access—Are victims able to find and use services when needed?

Structure—Are the needed services available and supported with a sustainable organization?

Process—Are victims treated respectfully, as unique individuals?

Outcomes—Are victims' situation and feelings improved from the services provided?

The answer to these four questions is the bridge from compassion to practice and from vision to application. If we are committed and passionate about helping crime victims, we must at least do the minimum, which is "do no harm!" We need core victim service standards, training, and curriculum to help us improve the lives of victims, regardless of whether they report the crime. Wherever and whenever the crime takes place, and whether advocates focus on the culpability of individual offenders or the larger societal and cultural injustices that cause crime, we need guidelines for victim services that address their needs.

We cannot perfectly know or understand a victim's situation, but we can work wisely. We can find our best efforts somewhere between art and science, between gut reactions and trained skills, and between each victim's unique responses and our common human reactions. Understanding quality begins with a cultural move away from focusing on our work, activities, programs, and a definition of quality as error reduction, toward emphasizing the change, impact, and outcome for the victim that results from our work. Victim outcome attainment levels are

---

Victim Recovery: Every Victim Every Time

If a 99.9% rate is OK, then:

- 12 babies to wrong parents daily is OK

- 2 unsafe airplanes at O'Hare daily is OK

- 315 misspelled words in Webster's is OK

- 20,000 incorrect drug prescriptions hourly is OK

- 880,000 faulty credit card charges daily is OK

You can't do the same thing over and over and expect different results

our report cards.

The distinction between a work focus and a victim-outcome focus is crucial. It is not *what* you do that is most important. Rather, it is the results of your actions that are vital. Working harder or more efficiently is wasted effort unless it correlates to the improvement in victims' lives, which they desire, and helps them move from surviving to thriving.

Improving the quality and impact of victim services and creating plans and measuring progress is not a job just for experts ("Nonprofit Organizational Effectiveness," 2006; Panel on the Nonprofit Sector, 2005). Every program leader who is trying to improve staff and services is already doing evaluation, and there are quality guides for doing so in an organized method (Consolidated Victim Service Program Standards, 2009).

What are we trying to measure?

You probably wonder sometimes if you are providing the right services or if your services are effective in improving victims' lives (Brickman, 2002). Research assistance is wonderful. With or without expert help, however, you still need to figure out your program goal and how to measure progress. The processes of determining your goal, and measuring your progress are critical (Burt, Harrell, Newmark, Aron, & Jacobs, 1997). You cannot skip these steps. The good news is that knowing your goal and your measuring sticks may be your most important strides, especially if you are new to the evaluation process. This guide provides ideas about what and how to measure victim service programs, from which you will be able to adapt your own tools for your own situations.

Whatever you want to accomplish, you want your effort and expertise to make a positive difference in victim's lives. If you know the core needs of victims, you can begin to figure out your particular goals, strategies, and success indicators. A good program design is one in which quantity and quality of work can be measured. Quality victim advocacy is ultimately measured by the degree to which victims' lives are improved. However, Victim Advocates cannot control the choices of victims or the variables of each situation. Furthermore, they cannot (without research) verify any linkage between their efforts and victims' outcomes.

It is certainly easier to measure work volume and sequence than it is to measure impact of outcomes. For example, a charting system can verify that a victim received a victim impact statement and that it was correctly submitted in a timely fashion during the court process. Similarly, adequate and acceptable shelter space is observable, as are the number and hours of staff training. It is harder to measure whether completing a victim impact statement provided the maximum emotional and justice benefit possible for that victim. How do you measure the quality of intervention provided by each staff member for each victim? We cannot account for the influencing factors within and surrounding the victim. We cannot presume causality. But we can account for our efforts and victim reported changes. The administrative principle applies: "If you did not document it, it did not happen." The measures that count, even if not perfect, are those that document the degree to which *victims' needs* are met.

> *Quality victim advocacy is ultimately measured by the degree to which victims' lives are improved.*

What are the indicators of a quality organization?

Organizational evaluation can take the form of the four diagnostic areas: access, structure, process, and outcomes. Each has indicators to help measure its strength in an organization. What does it mean for victims to have **access** to your program, to have the right services ready for them in your program **structure**, to have sensitive treatment by program personnel in the **process** of receiving services, and to have their lives changed by attaining their desired **outcomes**?

Access—victims know about, can find, and are able to use services

Victims must know about, be able to find, and utilize victim services. Underused services, however wonderfully designed, are wasteful. Victims need to know services are available at the moment they are needed. Since so many victims do not report crimes to law enforcement, and may not tell family and friends, victim services need to be well known and reputable to the public, allied professions, clergy, school officials, and others to whom victims may turn.

The core access issues include whether the victim advocacy services are:

1. Visible
   a. Are services known to the public through various media, such as television and radio public service announcements, billboards, posters at high-volume shopping and pedestrian areas, underserved population locations (e.g. gas stations, grocery stores, schools, libraries, doctors' offices, hair salons), booths at health fairs and malls, phone book ads, high schools, college campuses, etc.?
   b. Do referral sources know about, value, and inform victims of services, such as law enforcement, prosecutors, clergy, emergency room staff, mental health clinicians, health departments, school personnel, etc.?
   c. Can passersby see the facility's outdoor signage 24 hours a day (e.g. lit at night, easily readable, noticeable) and does it include basic information (e.g. phone number, web site, victims' needs addressed)?
2. Accessible
   a. Are services in the victim's community and offered to them (Stark, 2000)?
   b. Are services close to mass transit, parking, and identifiable landmarks?
   c. Are services near the legal, mental health, medical partners, justice officials and courthouses that victims need?
   d. Are the services and facilities accessible to persons with different languages, physical limitations, and limited English proficiency?
   e. Are services reachable 24 hours a day?
   f. Are intake staff qualified and intake procedures seamless for victims to reach the needed service providers?
3. Acceptable
   a. Are the atmosphere and tone of the facility warm? Are furnishings and decór comfortable, visually and culturally diverse? Are seating arrangements conducive to the flow of personal contact with staff?

Measuring Quality

ACCESS
Can victims find services?

PROCESS
Are victims treated respectfully?

STRUCTURE
Do services match victims' needs?

OUTCOMES
Are victims' lives improved?

With safety, healing, justice, and restitution

ACCESS

Visible—Media and community visibility

Accessible—Limited English Proficiency and Sign Language

Acceptable—Generous office hours and friendly staff

Available—Sufficient phone lines and e-mail options

b. Do victims perceive each staff contact as supportive and warm, staff voice tone, words, and nonverbal communications positive?

c. Are all interactions and their locations protective of victims' safety, privacy, and confidentiality?

d. Do the conclusion of services by phone, mail, in-person, e-mail, or other methods leave the victim feeling cared about and encouraged to contact services again?

4. Available

a. Are eligibility, jurisdiction, and assistance boundaries clear and known so victims can find the right services without undue hassle?

b. Can victims enter, navigate, and exit services easily (e.g. phone lines not busy, no waiting in lines, sufficient and understandable responses for their specific need provided by staff)?

c. Is the capacity of services equal to the demand so that requests result in prompt services when needed, such as emergency shelter, crisis counseling, case status, etc.?

d. Are website and e-mail service options possible, and are prompt responses received when contacted?

The initial contact with victims is the first place for victim services to avoid re-victimizing them.

Access to victim services is about trying to ensure that our customers can reach services efficiently and seamlessly and determine what, if any, services or options they need. Victims do not schedule or plan ahead for their trauma and violation. Crime is never convenient and happens while the victim's life is rushing forward. The initial contact with victims is the first place for victim services to avoid re-victimizing them.

Retail stores constantly advertise, even though the public may know their business location and hours. The lesson for victim services is to persist in publicizing services. A common and often cheap method of publicity is the use of free public service announcements on radio, television, billboards, public transportation, and in print media. Besides the traditional donation of space and time by the media, another method is to "piggy back" with a small ad box or tag line on business and other partner advertisements, such as local hospitals or cell phone providers. Place posters and brochure displays at law enforcement and social service agencies, hospitals, doctors' offices, and other responder locations in heavily trafficked stores to aid public education. Free media coverage of events, letters to the editor, news interviews, and related visual coverage of Victim's Rights Week or memorial events can be good public reminders of victim services. Neighborhood associations, civic clubs, places of worship, and other events offering public speaking opportunities are also valuable. An informative newsletter provides related professionals with reminders of how and why referrals are useful to victim services. Large print, lighted, and concise signage with contact information is an important communication tool.

The highest priority is victim security and confidentiality. This includes such issues as warnings at web site access points about tracking software, safe contact methods, and security measures for use of courtroom, shelter, and work places. Other areas to consider include visibility of victim files in offices, accessible information (without a security block) on the program data system, visible information on staff computer monitors, and trails left by victims of their Internet searches.

Some service entry and delivery points require monitoring, including 24 Hour crisis lines' dependability, toll-free options, and alternative language and hearing-impaired contact availability. Victim services' partners are also doorways to other services. Each must be explored for their unique accessibility issues (e.g. cultural and language differences). Some considerations for adapting advocacy services include hours of availability by phone, facility, texting, telecommunications device for the deaf (TDD), and e-mail.

Of course, funding restrictions limit the perfect access to services for every victim. Some necessary adaptations may include response messages sent immediately while victims hold or wait for a short time. Any delay, however, is unacceptable to some victims. Using technology for home-based response is appropriate in some cases, and may address the problem of adequate staffing for unpredictable "peak demand" moments while maintaining 24 hour response personnel.

Assuring victim-friendly and accessible services is important. A sigh on the phone, abruptness, a hint of irritation, or any interruption taints the trust and support victims need. Remember the saying "you don't get a second chance to make a good first impression." Do victims get the sense that the focus of the agency is the comfort and convenience of the staff or of the victim? When a caller asks what the agency does, is the answer simply a list of services he or she must comprehend and try to fit into? Or, is the response a short victim-centered summary of common needs followed by the question, "What would be helpful for you?" Phone lines ringing busy or having disruptive static, unreturned messages, and calls cut off during transfers indicate a lack of concern for victims and reflect poor service performance.

Similarly, are service hours convenient for victims? Are normal business hours dependable? Service availability hours should mirror the needs of victims in the jurisdiction, such as manufacturing, hospital, and restaurant shift work, school and campus schedules, and other unique community situations. For many people, a user-friendly website with safety warnings and service contact information is a valuable 24 hour access point.

Updated collaboration agreements and referral processes as well as regular cross training of partner agencies' staff are important, though less visible, strategies that help victims flow smoothly into services. Similarly, participation in justice, victim service, crime prevention, and community needs assessment collaborations and research result in information that is critical to creating responses that address unique local victim outcomes.

Access is being denied victims if services are not known, the agency cannot be reached, or a message is otherwise conveyed that services are not welcoming or victim-centered.

A sigh on the phone, abruptness, a hint of irritation, or any interruption taints the trust and support victims need.

	Victim Access Audit	5 Good	4 OK	3 -	2 Poor	1 Bad
1. **Visible**	Known to the public (e.g. 50% of people entering a grocery)					
2.	Known to referral sources (e.g. all law enforcement)					
3.	Covered monthly in media: billboards; TV; radio; newspaper					
4.	Web site user friendly: good links and design; useful content					
5.	Signage: lighted; contact information/hours; and Web site					
6. **Accessible**	Close to victim's community (e.g. 80% of victims say services are close enough to use)					
7.	Program is near transportation and parking					
8.	Program is near courthouse and service partners					
9.	Building, services, and offices physically accessible					
10.	Languages, Limited English Proficiency, TDD, and large print					
11.	24/7 crisis line and response to hospital and law enforcement					
12.	24/7 response to crime scene and for death notification					
13.	Seamless transition between 1st contact and services					
14. **Acceptable**	Friendly and warm facility, furnishings, and decorations					
15.	Voice tone, words and non-verbal greeting are friendly					
16.	Intake area private, confidential and safe					
17.	Conclusion of initial contact inviting and personal					
18.	Contact is culturally specific					
19. **Available**	Clear eligibility and services so victims find it on 1st try					
20.	Shelter, appointment and services ready when needed					
21.	Phone lines open and answered with right information					
22.	E-mail and website contact offered with prompt response					

Quality Area 2 of 4

STRUCTURE

Governance—Updated policies and audit

Parnterships—Active collaborations and protocols

Tools—Good data management and notices

Staff—Dedicated and expert staff

Services—Wide range and unique services

Structure—the right framework for the right victim services

Incorrect services, however wonderfully operated, cannot help victims meet their needs. Rating high in this area means the program is providing the services that victims need, sustained by an effective and efficient organization with diligent oversight (Checklist for Accountability, 2005). Structure is a more hidden component of quality.

The two primary pieces of a good structure include having the right services and the right design to implement and govern programs and services. A needs assessment, completed every five to seven years with input from justice and elected officials, victims, program board and staff, partners, and the public, is an important way to hear and determine victim and partner needs. Special attention must be paid to changing demographics, language, and other special and new victim populations.

Award-winning services that only meet the needs of a small percentage of victims are valuable, but should not overshadow the service needs of the majority of victims. Certainly many programs must provide specialized services to meet particular victim needs. Those promising practices should be recognized and duplicated without losing sight of an integrated program focused on its broader

Filling the Gaps

Structure
Design and Resources

<u>Victims</u>	<u>Prosecution</u>	<u>Services</u>	<u>Collaborative</u>
Sexual Assault	Felony	Court advocacy	Legal Aid
Domestic Violence	Misdemeanor	Hotlines	Task Forces
Identity	Juvenile	Spiritual Services	Counseling
Homicide	Unsolved	Death Notices	Forensic Nurses
Violent	Unreported	Repairs and Shelter	Interpreters
Property	Parole/Probation	Protection Orders	Disabilities
Trafficking	International	Transportation	Prevention

vision and mission.

Many additional issues influence whether an organization is well designed and operated (i.e. governed) and to which victim service organizations must be vigilant and adaptable. Good governance includes many issues that are beyond the few key items mentioned in this guide (The Principals Workbook, 2009, Authenticity Consulting LLC, 2008). For example, a regular review of changes in local and state policies and/or legislation may require new or adjusted services, such as changing the roles of victims and their needs for support or information in the state parole process or the local/regional parole violation process. Additionally, has the victim compensation program changed the application process, victim eligibility, or provider payment method? Has new law enforcement or prosecutor leadership changed the way crimes are charged or bail recommendations determined? Have judges, jail over-crowding, or leadership changes varied the jail trustee system so inmates are released early or allowed work privileges outside the jail? How are victims and victim advocacy organizations included in a timely manner on court cases, inmate releases, or system changes? Have any incidents in a local community or high publicity cases regionally discouraged certain victims from seeking help? Not only are victim service organizations complex, but so are the larger political, media, and justice systems with which victim services must stay in sync.

Basic structure decisions include determining which victims are the highest priorities, the period for service provision, and the type of needs that funding, expertise, facility, and other factors allow. The needs of felony, misdemeanor, juvenile, unsolved, and unreported crime victims vary widely. Besides funding and staffing issues, the ability to provide advocacy through collaborations that expand the timing, quality, types, and length of services will affect what services victims end up receiving. Task forces and partnerships can expand services and provide the specificity needed. For example, some important partnerships include mental and developmentally disabled programs, Forensic Nurse Examiners, legal aid, interpreters, mental health agencies, as well as youth runaway, adult, and family homeless shelters.

The structural design for staff positions, training, monitoring, evaluation, and coaching can make all the difference in having competent and productive

Not only are victim service organizations complex, but so are the larger political, media, and justice systems with which victim services must stay in sync.

staff and volunteers who focus on meeting victims' needs. Critical personnel issues include board members, directors, and managers providing:

1. Staff training and career development opportunities
2. Positive and timely communication and coaching
3. Praise and rewards for meritorious service
4. Positive atmosphere and accountability for poor performers
5. Kind and firm supervision and policy enforcement
6. Adequate equipment, supplies, and work space
7. Respect and legitimacy from allied professionals
8. Reasonable workloads
9. Vision, praise, and guidance on attaining victim outcomes
10. Reasonable pay and benefits

Hidden from public view are the structural issues.

Hidden from public view are the structural issues of maintaining fiscal checks and balances, working within a fixed budget, ensuring a clean audit, timely and accurate paying of taxes and Internal Revenue Service filings, and providing adequate insurance coverage for professional, office, and vehicle liabilities. The ability to find, write, implement, and comply with grants is also essential (Internal Revenue Service, 2009).

Other organizational components of a solid program structure include, for example, the ability to create and sustain fund raising events, follow ethical values, maintain dependable services, and preserve a leadership culture that consistently listens and explains decisions and goals to staff and stakeholders. This open culture respects questions, values documentation, recognizes accomplishments, and prioritizes an environment of both encouragement and accountability (Principles and Practices, 2005).

Avoiding disasters is the minimum test of a good structure. Some extreme examples:

1. Hiring the wrong staff (e.g. hiring a sex offender to help sexual assault victims)
2. Losing organizational computer data (e.g. not having a daily out-of-the-office back-up system in case of fire, vandalism, water damage, computer failure, etc.)
3. Violating victim and staff safety (e.g. not having security procedures in place, violating confidentiality)
4. Financial ruin or penalties (e.g. from non-payment of taxes, cancellation of insurance due to ignoring recommendations in prior audit management letters, failure to pay unemployment or workers compensation)

In summary, some core structure issues include whether the victim advocacy framework includes appropriate:

1. Governance
   a. Is funding adequate and the core budget stable (with less than 10% variance from year to year)?
   b. Are financial checks and balances and document retention policies approved and followed?
   c. Is the oversight board providing due diligence, leadership, and loyalty?

In a system-based program, does the supervising official provide independence and confidentiality for victim-centered advocacy?

d. Is the director evaluated annually with in-depth review and specific guidance?

e. Does the program have a clear mission, with services linked to it?

f. Is a needs assessment completed every 5-7 years, and then services adapted to results?

g. Are annual reviews conducted of policies, job duties, and manuals?

2. Partnerships

a. Are program-crossing files, data, and services available when needed?

b. Is the collaboration regularly reviewing the "big picture" system process?

c. Does the program do media releases, reports, and events for publicity?

d. Is there opportunity for volunteers, interns, and civic clubs to assist?

e. Are legal, spiritual, counseling, medical, disabilities, and language partners connected?

f. Are collaboration protocols clear, monitored, and updated with partners?

3. Tools

a. Are the computer and copier equipment, phone system, Internet speed, and work space (e.g. illumination, noise, efficiency) adequate?

b. Are program confidentiality policies and security protections updated?

c. Is material victim-specific (e.g. trauma, compensation, court process)?

d. Is the data management system efficient, fast, and dependable?

e. Are quality and outcome evaluation participation rates increasing (over 50% of victims served), and victim positive response rates at least 80%?

4. Staff

a. Are staff qualified, insightful, intelligent, honest, hard working, dependable, mutually supportive, and racially and ethnically reflective of the community?

b. Are staff encouraged to quality for national credentialing and to understand and follow national service standards?

c. Are there regular staff meetings, annual evaluations, and reward perks?

d. Is pay for staff reasonable and the turnover rate less than 15% annually?

e. Is there a program-wide culture of caring, professionalism, and fun?

f. Is staff provided annual cultural diversity, ethics, and trauma training?

g. Is staff outcome knowledge and utilization reviewed regularly?

5. Services

a. Are services comprehensive, appropriate, and linked to an outcome?

b. Do service design and staff assignments prioritize the same number of staff per victim?

c. Is emergency money available for crisis needs (e.g. utilities, locks)?

d. Is there outreach to unreported, disabled, and at-risk victim populations?

Is staff outcome knowledge and utilization reviewed regularly?

Structural integrity includes providing the services actually needed, and sustaining a meaningful communication system with staff and partners, and a review process for the facility and organizational procedures. ***The key to maintaining structural integrity is in monitoring and revising.*** In other words, is someone reviewing and addressing the program components and linkages? For example, are the data management issues of speed (e.g. finding victim data) and efficiency (e.g. needing to re-key victim data) considered and improved?

	Program Structure Audit	5 good	4 OK	3 -	2 Poor	1 Bad
1. **Governance**	Stable budgets with annual and strategic planning practiced					
2.	Financial checks and balances in policy and practice plus an annual audit					
3.	Expert oversight Board that meets regularly with a quorum					
4.	Board evaluates director annually and all donate to the program					
5.	Clear mission focus linked to programs and services					
6.	Needs assessment every 5-7 years with partners and public					
7.	Access-Structure-Process-Outcome audit every 2 years					
8.	Updated policies, job duties, and organizational chart					
9. **Partnerships**	Access to police, prosecutor, and court files (read-only)					
10.	Protocol in place and reviewed quarterly for justice quality					
11.	Monthly media release, public event, or newsletter					
12.	Volunteer program for community members and interns					
13.	Legal, spiritual, counseling, medical, and language links					
14. **Tools**	Good equipment, Internet speed, software and work areas					
15.	Confidentiality and security protections for victims and staff					
16.	User-friendly victim rights and trauma recovery material					
17.	Data management: speed, accuracy, reports, and back-up					
18.	Quality and outcome evaluations used with increasing returns					
19. **Staff**	Positive, expert, work ethic, documentation, reflect community					
20.	Priority of national credentialing and service standards					
21.	Monthly staff meetings, annual evaluations and anniversary awards					
22.	Reasonable staff pay and turnover rate of less than 15%					
23.	Culture of caring, professionalism, collaboration and fun					
24.	Annual job specific, diversity, ethics, and trauma trainings					
25.	Semi-annual outcome review and progress plan for all staff					
26.	Evaluated for outcome knowledge, use, and improvements					
27. **Services**	Comprehensive services linked to victim outcomes					
28.	Advocacy designed for helping from crime to victim recovery					
29.	Emergency money for medicine, utilities, locks, etc.					
30.	Outreach to unreported, disabled, at-risk and prior victims					

Process—respectful treatment of victims while in services

Accessible and appropriate services that are not provided in a respectful manner to the victim are serious deviations from the mission. The treatment of victims with fairness, dignity, and respect is enshrined in many state constitutions and laws. Victims differ in their ability to understand and accept services even when sincere efforts are made to communicate with them effectively.

Victim sensitive service depends on good listening skills, an ability to walk beside each victim, and the insight to respond appropriately to the unique cultural, trauma, and victimization situation. This includes timely and accurate safety, healing, justice, and financial recovery information. The same Victim Advocate should provide services (vertical advocacy); substitutions by coworkers that may happen should be the exception and not the rule. All programs must prioritize safety, including physical security and maintaining the confidentiality of information throughout the intake and service processes.

Programs with good process components will not only benefit victims with unique, warm, and empathetic treatment, but the programs will gain information more quickly about issues important to victims (Tewksbury, Moore, & King, 1998). For example, victims who feel respected will share concerns about the program and partner service systems (e.g. legal aid, mental health, hospital, justice system). Good listening is foundational. Notice when a victim asks for information already provided. Improve the communication issue by offering information in writing, graciously repeating it more simply or slowly, giving information in a different sequence, or providing it at a different time in the case progression. Simple, honest, and concise explanations and questions are best.

Some core process issues include whether services are provided in a manner that is:

1. Ethical (National Standards Manual, sc.edu, 9/9/09).
   a. Does staff adhere to Ethical Standards for Victim Assistance Providers? Are victims' safety and self-determination the highest priority?
   b. Are victims' civil, legal, and personal rights consistently respected?
   c. Is a respectful and timely grievance process offered?
2. Professional
   a. Are information and hearing notice contacts accurate and timely?
   b. Is material understandable, in large font, and as pictorial as possible?
   c. Do staff dress and act respectfully toward victims, the victimization, and officials?
   d. Are victims prepared for meetings, hearings, and offender contacts?
   e. As appropriate, are restorative justice options provided?
3. Unique
   a. Is cultural sensitivity conveyed in word, deed, and the surroundings?
   b. Are faith issues raised, and concerns responded to promptly?
   c. Are victims' biases, questions, interests, and special needs accepted?
   d. Is each victim's story listened whenever needed and acknowledged?
   e. Are victims' fears and security concerns (real or perceived) prioritized?
   f. Are services and treatment plans victim driven and updated?

Quality Area 3 of 4

PROCESS

Ethical—Privacy and security protected

Professional—Respect and care prioritized

Unique—Victim driven services and choices

Sensitive—Cultural and faith awareness

4. Sensitive

    a. Is advocacy both victim-specific and addressing larger system problems?

    b. Are victims provided the same advocate from contact until case closing?

    c. Is response for help timely, on-task, dependable, and respectful?

    d. Are victims provided an open-ended and warm invitation to return?

    e. As appropriate, are follow-up contacts made (especially in cases of severe violence)?

Treating victims as valued customers and as the primary guide for services is the right approach and response. Each person deserves a culturally sensitive, user-friendly, and safe environment.

	Victim Process Audit	5 Good	4 OK	3 -	2 Poor	1 Bad
1. **Ethical**	Ethical Standards for Victim Assistance Providers followed					
2.	Victim safety and self-determination the highest priority					
3.	Victim civil, legal, and personal rights consistently respected					
4.	Respectful and timely grievance process provided					
5. **Professional**	Accurate and timely notices and information provided					
6.	Information understandable, large font, and pictorial when possible					
7.	Dress code and attitude reflect the seriousness of victimization					
8.	Victim prepared for meetings, hearings and offender contacts					
9.	Restorative justice options provided, as appropriate					
10. **Unique**	Cultural sensitivity in word, deed, and surroundings					
11.	Faith issues addressed and concerns assisted promptly					
12.	Victims' interests, biases and special needs accepted					
13.	Victims' story listened to whenever needed and acknowledged					
14.	Focus on actual and perceived victim security needs					
15.	Victim-driven treatment plan and victim choice of services					
16. **Sensitive**	Advocacy for victims' personal needs and system changes					
17.	Same advocate for victim from contact to case closing					
18.	Responsive and empathetic contacts and assistance					
19.	Open-ended case closing encouraging for victims to re-contact					
20.	Care card sent on anniversary date of violence—as appropriate					

Outcomes—changes in victim's lives

The goal of victim services is to support victims in their desire for a positive change in attitudes, insights, knowledge, and/or a modified behavior, an improved condition, an altered status, or an increased skill. An outcome can be defined as the positive result the victim desires in order to solve a problem or address a need (Zweig, et al, 2003). For example, if a victim needs to pay a crime-related debt, the outcome the victim desires is to have the bill paid.

A victim is not better off simply because program staff work harder or reach high productivity levels. Rather, success is reaching a victim's desired improvements. You do not make a difference in someone's life just by providing him or her with a service. Rather, you make a difference by helping them achieve changes in their lives that they choose. Providing victims with hearing notifications may actually be harmful if Victim Advocates do not also prepare the victim for the hearing and the justice process, or ensure the victim's right to be informed, present, and heard by system officials. The victim service outcome can be defined as a victim having a need met. For example, a victim's need for a healing and justice outcome often means having his or her victimization acknowledged, having their story heard, being able to witness someone taking responsibility for the crime (or observe the culpability being placed on someone), and having their views of fair consequences seriously considered.

The needs of victims are our outcome targets. Like a business, you want your customer to utilize your services because they believe you can meet their needs. Our business plan is to meet victim needs, not make a profit. All the components of an organization should link to make a change in a victim's life.

Services must be logically connected to accomplishing a particular victim outcome and benefit. You help a victim get a protection order because you care about the victim's SAFETY. You provide crisis intervention to improve the victim's emotional HEALING. You tell a victim about hearings so he or she can be present, heard, and feel that JUSTICE is being done. You help a victim file for victim compensation or seek reimbursement from the perpetrator so the victim is financially RESTITUTED.

The measure of success and quality is ultimately the degree to which a victim's need is met in the areas of safety, healing, justice, and restitution (financial recovery to pre-crime level). Programs should measure their policies and practices against these four outcome goals. The goal of victim advocacy programs is to provide the unique services necessary for each victim to improve in one or more of the areas they have need.

Safety needs are the highest priority. Meeting this need is never 100% certain, since offender characteristics, law enforcement response, prison escapes, and many other variables enter into the safety equation. Some of the services which may be provided include offender custody and release information, emergency shelter, protection orders (civil and criminal), repairing locks and doors, providing emergency cell phones, requesting increased law enforcement patrols, and encouraging involvement and support from trusted family and friends.

Healing needs are unique for each victim. The primary areas of concern are usually emotional, spiritual, and physical needs. The needs of victims vary greatly, for example, between victims of trafficking, armed robbery, and I.D. theft. Victims may heal psychologically through their own resilience and/or with support from friends, family, co-workers, clergy, and counselors. The role of victim services is often to provide crisis counseling, connect with medical diagnosis and treatment, refer to clergy, offer on-going counseling or a support group, and provide a caring listening ear. Another role is to improve friends and family support by helping them understand that healing is a process and that there may be many kinds of emotional triggers for victims. Caring people need to avoid asking,

Quality Area 4 of 4

OUTCOMES

Safety—Actual and perceived security

Healing—Emotional, spiritual, and medical recovery

Justice—System fairness, rights, and respect

Restitution—Financial recovery and stability

"What is wrong?," and instead ask "Would you like to talk about it?"

Victims define **justice** differently. For many victims, justice is absolution and fair resolution. Victims want to tell their stories and hear confirmation of their innocence and violation, and know that consequences are accepted by or imposed on the perpetrator. Considering that many victims do not report the crimes to police, and that prosecution of the offenders is often not possible, often means justice is defined differently by victims. Applicable laws, jurisdiction and extradition problems, investigation levels, prosecutors' decisions, alternative sentencing options, offender choices, available evidence, and other issues complicate finding each victim their form of justice. Victim services which address justice concerns may include investigation status, serving as liaison between victim and law enforcement, arrest or summons information, advocacy with investigators and prosecutors, advocacy during the court process, timely and accurate hearing notices, witness support, and serving as post-sentence liaison with probation, parole, custody institutions, halfway houses, and other entities.

Victims are most likely to disclose **financial recovery** (restitution) needs, but attaining full recovery is much less frequent. Victims can have emergency, ongoing, or longterm financial concerns as a result of the crimes. The ripple effect of crime may include their inability to work physically and emotionally, as well as loss of pay due to crime-related absences injuries, court hearings, and other recovery requirements. Financial impacts can include such items such as medical, security, counseling, childcare, housing, transportation, travel, and document replacement expenses.

Each state's victim compensation program is also a resource for most injured victims. Some provide limited assistance for property lost, damaged, or taken for evidence purposes. Court ordered restitution in the form of repayment to victims by offenders is common. Victim services often play a role in documenting and submitting amounts that victims or providers (car repair shops, insurance company, etc.) are owed. Civil law suits may also be an option for victims' financial recovery (National Victim Bar Association, 2009).

OUTCOMES—making a difference in victims' lives –

Attaining victim outcomes is why victim services exist. Victim's needs are unique, but victims may need one or more of the four primary areas. Sample survey items/actions:

For many victims, justice is absolution and fair resolution

Victim Outcome Audit
SAFETY—Actual and perceived
1. *This program has helped make me more aware of my safety options*
HEALING - Emotional, spiritual and physical
2. *I have a better understanding of my crisis and trauma*
3. *I feel less alone since working with this program*
4. Victims know if they were a crime victim (assessment by staff, not victim)
JUSTICE system fairness, rights, and respect
5. *I have a better understanding of how the justice process works*
6. *I know more about my legal rights since working with this program*
RESTITUTION and financial stability
7. *I know about the state Victim Compensation for victims of violent crime*
OUTCOME FOCUSED ACTIONS—use ranking of 5 (good)—4—3—2—1 (bad)
8. Hiring ads and event announcements note victim outcomes
9. Hiring interviews include outcome implementation questions and role play
10. Staff meetings include staff reports and recognition for outcome successes
11. Facility posts up-to-date and publicizes victim outcome measure results
12. Media interviews, fundraising events and speeches include outcome stories
13. Victim outcomes and mission statement are prominently posted in facility
14. Activity manual created and used correlating services to victim outcomes
15. Staff training related to intended outcome improvement
16. Annual evaluation of jobs, pay, and equipment/software linked to outcomes
17. Inter-agency collaborations created and monitored for better outcomes
18. Outcomes compared with similar programs and reported to staff and board
19. Victim and donor communication and program reports focus on outcomes
20. Annual and strategic planning centered on outcomes, plus plan for improvement
21. Grants, service and collaboration requests evaluated by impact on outcomes
22. Journal kept of changes impacting outcomes: staff, duties, protocols, procedures
23. Marketing themes are victim outcome oriented
24. Program services and reporting centered on Initial outcomes
25. Outputs reports of service quantity linked to positively impacted outcomes
26. Volunteer recruitment and recognition focused on positively impacted outcomes
27. Prevention of crimes and re-victimizations recognized as long-term outcomes
28. Outcome specific stories provided grant and funding sources
29. Program novelty and publicity items (e.g. shirts, pens) convey outcome focus
30. *SATISFACTION: I am satisfied with the services I received from this program*

**OUTCOMES—making a difference in victim's lives –
More sample victim outcome survey items**

	SAMPLE EVALUATION ITEMS **left** justified below asked of victim; **right** justified below completed by program
Access	*I was able to contact this program when needed*
Visible	Quarterly media or public event
Accessible	Access to interpreter or language help within 2 minutes
Acceptable	*The program space helped me feel comfortable & secure*
Available	Phone calls answered by 2rd ring by knowledgeable staff
Structure	*The services I needed were available at, or through, this program*
Governance	Board meets monthly with quorum
Partnerships	Partners provide outcome-measured services
Tools	Victim data management system on-line 98% of the time
Staff	Staff training documented and linked to outcomes
Services	One new service added annually
Process	*I was treated with respect by program staff*
Ethical	Program passes annual confidentiality audit
Professional	Material understandable, large font, and bi-lingual
Unique	Spiritual chaplain, clergy, or volunteers trained and available
Sensitive	Victims intake process uses self-selection of services
Outcomes	
Safety	*This program has helped make me more aware of my safety options*
	Emergency cell phones and emergency shelter available
Healing	*I feel less alone since working with this program*
	My trauma symptoms have been reduced *(Nightmares, flashbacks, anger, self-blame disorganization, etc.)*
	I have a better understanding of my crisis and trauma *I have a better understanding of the power and control wheel*
Justice	*I have a better understanding of how the justice process works*
	Advocate and accompany victims for each court hearing
	I know more about my legal rights since working with this program
Financial/Restitution	*I know about Victim Compensation for victims of violent crime*
	Emergency help is provided for new locks, medicine, and repairs
Satisfaction	*I am satisfied with the services I received from this program*

Is efficiency a quality issue?

Efficiency is a component of quality for all organizations. Program managers usually have enough data collected and tracked to measure cost-effectiveness. It is not a stretch to study efficiency. It is the challenge of trying to find the best coexistence among the right type, level, and volume of victim services, within limited resources, with imperfect information, and which reliably delivers victim outcomes. The goal may include:

1. Achieving consistently valuable outcome measures at the lowest possible cost of resources (e.g. money and time)
2. Measuring cost per activity or cost per output (Norman, Spencer, & Feder, 2007)
3. Maximizing the number of units of services from a fixed level of resources

However, efficiency is not always the most critical factor. For example, victim populations of homeless or mentally and developmentally disabled may be comparatively costly to reach and assist, but are still a priority. Additionally, issues of economics, ethics, and values also influence what is the *best* use of resources. For example, is it better to attempt to reduce the number of abused women who return to a violent relationship by investing in more programming (and less efficiency per person), or accept higher re-abuse relationships over time with a higher volume (and more efficiency) of women served? In other words, is eliminating violence in 75% of 100 people served better than reducing violence in 50% of 500 people served? You may need to clarify if your grantor or program's goal is to *efficiently* increase economic self-sufficiency, stabilize housing, lower medical costs, reduce criminal justice involvements and costs, or eliminate abuse?

Stakeholders want value. Victims, grantors, taxpayers, and donors want demonstrable, reportable, and compelling outcomes delivered to the right victims in a high quality and reliable manner at an acceptable cost. In other words, value means providing customer friendly access to the right services in an empowering manner that meets victim needs, while using the least expense of resources. Efficiency is the quality crown for programs reaching victim outcomes. It is like making sure that precious water is not leaking from its container on a desert hike.

Another way to discuss effective and efficient attainment of outcomes is to consider how quickly victims receive services and outcomes. For example, a victim that promptly receives many safety services is likely to feel safer sooner. Certainly, some services depend on other partners, such as the courts, for issuing protection orders. Courts may also be influenced by a victim service program submitting reports on the effectiveness of the courts' orders back to the court. Documentation of efficiency measures is instructive and useful for urging action by related entities. Some examples:

1. Safety—How soon are protection orders provided? What is the response time to repair or replace broken locks, doors, and windows?
2. Healing—How many meeting hours does it take before support group members complete the power and control wheel questionnaire at 95% or above? How soon do victims internalize the message that the crime was not their fault?
3. Justice—How soon is the victim's voice heard in the justice system? How

Calculating efficiency is similar to figuring miles per gallon.

Some examples:

1. Access—Victim contact attempts per successes at accessing services
2. Structure—Staff FTEs (full time equivalent) hours per victims assisted
3. Process—Notice accuracy per hearing notices provided
4. Outcomes—Staff Intervention hours per reduced trauma symptoms

Pop Quiz: Quality Areas

1. Confidentiality protected on computer screens

2. Dentist receives Victim Compensation check

3. VOCA grant increase allows new court service

4. Victim finds 24 hour phone number on website

Choose the correct program issue for each action.

1. _____   a. Access

2. _____   b. Structure

3. _____   c. Process

4. _____   d. Outcomes

Answers:

1. Process—Maintaining confidentiality of victim's data on office computer screens by preventing it from being seen by people walking past is a safety and respectful treatment issue.

2. Outcome—The victim's condition is improved since there is now no debt to the dentist for the crime related injury.

3. Structure—Adding new services improves the design of the program to attain victim outcomes, following the activity of writing a successful Victims of Crime Act (VOCA) grant.

4. Access—The program was visible since its web site provided a victim with information and was accessible with a 24 hours contact service when needed.

soon are victims provided victim service staff or attorneys to appeal actions when the justice, medical, or social systems fail to respond or respond inappropriately?

4. Restitution—How long before Victims Compensation is received (not just filed)? How soon is the first restitution payment received (e.g. by taking restitution from offender bond money, requiring that it be paid before court costs and fines)?

Chapter 1 Summary: Designing Victim-Focused Quality

The four components of quality victim advocacy are: Access—victim services being visible, accessible (reachable), acceptable, and available; Structure—the right victim services provided by a program designed with good governance, partnerships, tools, and staff; Process—victim treatment that is ethical, professional, uniquely provided, and sensitive); and Outcomes—meeting victim-directed needs of safety, healing, justice, and financial recovery (restitution to pre-crime levels). Each quality area can be measured for appropriate implementation, effectiveness, and efficiency.

Chapter 2
Understanding Outcomes

No outcomes, no direction
Know outcomes, know how to help

What is an outcome?

What is your answer when you are asked the question, "How is your program doing?" Do you note how many victims you helped, describe a new grant or program, or tell a heart-warming story about how you touched a victim's life? Stories are powerful because people can identify with real problems and their noticeable improvements. Positive stories resulting from our services reflect the "product quality" of victim advocacy. From a victim saying, "I didn't know what to do," to later saying, "Now I know," or, "Now I feel safe," is music to our ears. Listening carefully to victims needs and redoubling our effort when a victim says, "You don't understand," is at the core of victim advocacy excellence. Victims are the owners of the change. We provide the avenue, but the victims decide whether and how much to take advantage of the services.

The word outcome is often defined as "the sum of," as in, "the outcome of adding two plus two is four." However, in the victim advocacy context, an *outcome* is a change in a victim's life that they desire. For example, we do not make a difference in a victim's life simply by operating a support group. A support group is a valuable service if in the end the participants experience the intended changes. It is the support group environment, member participation, curriculum, leader techniques, and other factors that are the invitations for the survivors to change that may result in measurable improvements (outcomes) of their attitudes, behaviors, conditions, knowledge, insights, status, or skills.

Do victims have common outcomes?

Victims are unique, and each reacts differently to crime. No two victim advocacy programs are alike either. So, do commonalities exist?

- Are victims too dissimilar to share common outcomes?

- Can both system-based and community programs have common victim outcomes?

- Has anyone identified a few "universal outcomes" for crime victims?

Can you define service quality and find common victim needs?

- Are victims too different?

- Are system and community programs too different?

- Is there enough research?

- What measurement tools should be used?

- Can programs provide accurate data?

- Are crisis-oriented and long-term services too different?

- Who defines quality—victims or the program director?

41

- What measurement tools are available at the local program level to determine or measure victim outcomes?

- If multi-county programs have problems counting and defining services similarly, can we ever expect programs across the nation to gather useable and accurate data on victim changes?

- Are crisis calls and long-term services too dissimilar to reach similar outcomes?

- Who decides how to define quality and which victim outcome goals to try to reach? Do victims, Victim Advocates, or the largest funders (e.g. foundations, justice officials, financial sponsors, federal or state grant guidelines)? Or, do program directors, boards of directors, or elected officials operating victim programs define success?

Victim services have produced a body of knowledge about victims' common needs over the last 30 plus years. The movement has developed into a field. We can look back far enough to recognize pioneers of the field, such as the late Frank Carrington, our "Father of Victim Rights." We have growing numbers of journals and research publications, an alphabet soup of organizations and grants, as well as training centers, victimology educational degrees, and a growing market of goods and resources to assist the variety of victim service programs and specializations. It is time to recognize a few theses for success in victim advocacy.

As noted earlier, this guide generalizes and simplifies victim needs into four core areas. No matter the nature of the crime (e.g. theft of a child's toy, identity theft, rape, domestic violence, murder, terrorism, kidnapping), victim needs come in four categories. The core needs of victims are safety (individual physical well-being), healing (spiritual, emotional, medical, etc.), justice (participation, offender accountability, victimization acknowledgement, etc.), and financial stability/restitution (recovery through victim compensation, offender paid restitution, employment and housing assistance, etc.). All of these needs can exist regardless whether a case is being investigated by law enforcement and with or without the arrest of the offender(s).

Victims' experiences of violation, trauma, confusion, and loss can be understood within the issues of safety, healing, justice, and financial recovery.

In other words, a positive outcome in victim advocacy is defined as an improvement in a crime victim's life. Victims' experiences of violation, trauma, confusion, and loss can be understood within the issues of safety, healing, justice, and financial recovery. Some category differences may be semantic and some conceptual. In any case, our goal is to assure that victims' lives are improved—by the choices and decisions of victims—as we attempt to provide best-practice outreach to the wide range and special populations of victims, with the right services, and an optimal delivery process for each service.

The goal of victim advocacy programs is to operate with high quality access, structure, and process in order for victims to experience positive outcomes. The emphasis is not on the crime's label, but rather on the unique and self-identified needs of each victim. The path to recovery runs through the resilience and empowerment of victims who are encouraged with information, choices, and support in the areas of safety, healing, justice, and financial recovery.

Do outcomes fit with the U.S. Department of Justice's Global Challenges?

One strategic response to helping crime victims is the U.S. Department of Justice, Office for Victims of Crimes', "Five Global Challenges from the Field" (U.S. Department of Justice, 1998). They include:

1. To enact and enforce consistent, fundamental rights for crime victims
2. To provide crime victims with access to comprehensive, quality services
3. To integrate crime victims' issues into all levels of the nation's educational system
4. To support, improve, and replicate promising practices in victims' rights and services
5. To ensure that the voices of crime victims play a central role in the nation's response to violence

> **Cultural Change from Outputs to Outcomes**
>
> "In every program, and in every agency, we are measuring success not by good intentions, or by dollars spent, but rather by results achieved."
>
> U.S. Government Performance Results Act of 1994 and later Presidential budget messages

If we know the essential needs of victims and the necessary outcomes toward which we strive, then we can understand how to define success for each challenge. Achieving victim outcomes as our ultimate goal means that, for example:

1. The real success of enacted legal rights is whether those rights actually result in a benefit to victims; a legal right that is unavailable to a victim is not a "win"
2. The definition of comprehensive and quality services involves measuring program access, structure, process, and outcomes
3. The guide for what issues need to be integrated into victim advocate training and education will include quality and outcome areas
4. The measuring stick for assessing the quality of services is their outcome benefits for victims
5. A plum line for measuring success in reducing re-victimization is in empowering victims to attain:
   a. Improved safety
   b. Increased medical, spiritual, and emotional healing
   c. Improved sense of justice
   d. Increased ability to recover financially from crime-related costs

Does Federal funding address performance-based assessments?

National and state grants are moving toward measuring outcomes and using performance-based assessments. The U.S. Department of Justice, the source of Victims of Crime Act (VOCA) and Violence Against Women Act (VAWA) grants, have embraced the concept of performance-based management (U.S. Department of Justice, 2006). This is illustrated by the federal government assessing the VOCA program with the criterion: "Budget requests for the crime victims' programs need to be better justified by linking resources to expected results" (Detailed Information, 2006).

National and state grants are moving toward measuring outcomes and using performance-based assessments.

The specific list of federal government Program Performance Measures includes the five areas below, however, the use of the term "outcome" below is not necessarily a "victim outcome" as defined in this guide, and *bracketed and italicized comments are added by this author* [See Exhibit 1 for the full list] (Detailed Information, 2006).

1. Outcome Measure: Ratio of victims who received Crime Victims Fund assistance services to the total number of victimizations *{This is an output not an outcome measure, as defined by this guide, as it reflects work done by programs to provide a service and not a victim improvement by receiving the money.}*

2. Outcome Measure: Ratio of Crime Victims Fund compensation dollars awarded to total economic loss incurred by victims of crime *{This "ratio" indirectly reports that money is awarded victims, which is a financial outcome.}*

3. Output Measure: The number of victims who received Crime Victims Fund assistance services *{An output measure of work, as used in this guide}*

4. Outcome Measure: Percentage of violent crime victims who received help from victim service agencies *{An output measure, as defined in this guide, of services provided by programs and not life improvements in victims of violent crime}*

5. Efficiency Measure: Ratio of Crime Victims Fund dollars awarded to program management and administrative (M&A) dollars spent *{An efficiency measure related to inputs of money.}*

The U.S. Justice Department's Office for Victims of Crime (OVC) has considered an assessment tool to measure impact of services in victims' lives, collaborations, and in victim satisfaction with services. One draft submitted to OVC had 18 outcome measures from which local programs would select five measures appropriate to their particular victim service program (Derene, S., Bailey, J.D., Montagnino, S., 2004).

What is our anchoring principle?

Services are supposed to improve victims' lives. The intentions of most organizations sound good. The 1.6 million non-profit organizations in the United States (The Forbes Funds, 2004) have mission statements with some altruistic intentions, and many have clear goals and objectives to measure success. However, measuring goal attainment and demonstrating success in changing lives are two different measures unless goals are stated in victim outcome terms. For victim services, the barometer of success is being able to report impacts and improvements in victims' lives. For example, it is the difference between simply having a safety plan in place and having a safety plan that results in victims remaining safe.

Achieving victim outcomes require persistent leadership. It includes simple tasks like changing our "to do" list to one focusing on outcomes and charting victim-specific goals linked with tasks required to accomplish those goals. However, success is not getting an action list completed; it is changing the victims' world for the better.

Understanding the real needs of victims and assuring services that reach those outcomes is a critical ingredient of any holistic theory or philosophy of fairness and justice. For example, the concept of restorative justice views crime as a violation of *people*, not just a violation of *law*. This helpful worldview presumes that victims deserve parallel presumptions as the accused to innocence, protection, due process, rehabilitation, and to support as they search for safety, healing, justice, and financial recovery.

The victim field has named the anchors of victim rights in the proposed Victim Rights Amendment to the U.S. Constitution: to be informed; to be present; to be heard; to consideration of safety, to just and timely restitution; and with the notice and standing to enforce these rights (National Victims Constitutional Amendment Passage, 2003). Likewise, the larger pillars of victim advocacy that guide services are the core recovery needs for safety, healing, justice, and restitution. Providing a comprehensive approach allows victims to find the services and advocacy that are effective for them.

Understanding core victim needs creates a mission focus for victim service providers to develop new and more specialized services across the nation. A common understanding of essential victim needs provides a guide for training and services. Consensus on recovery outcomes will improve the victims' capacity for self-help strategies and provide guidance on developing outcome logic models. Paperback books, websites, and downloadable guides can promote victim knowledge and empowerment with, for example, "Victim Recovery for First-Timers," or "Choosing Your Safe-

> *However, measuring goal attainment and demonstrating success in changing lives are two different measures unless goals are stated in victim outcome terms.*

Victim Outcomes as Goals

Outcomes are changes in victims' attitudes, behaviors, conditions, knowledge, insights, status, and skills.

Outcomes are NOT expert staff, an increase in number of clients served, creation of support groups, or reduction in crime.

ty and Recovery Goals," or "Justice Process Tutorial for Victims" (Boland, 1997).

Knowing there is a recovery model can give hope to victims, as long as it is not prescriptive or a fixed process. The road to recovery is always personal. Victims who can recognize their own footprints in initial and crisis outcomes may feel their future is more hopeful as they look for their unique recovery path. As insightful and informed customers, victims can speed their knowledge and understanding of their situation. Like coming prepared to discuss options with a physician, informed victims can improve their choices and decisions. Informed victims also change the roles of the Victim Advocates. Advocates can spend less of their limited time simply explaining the sequence of events and more time listening for victims' unique outcome goals and assisting them toward those targets.

What is the difference between traditional and outcome measures?

Traditional measures of activities, outputs, effort, and compliance are often critical components of reaching victim outcomes. However, they are distinct, including:

The Question
Traditional: What service is provided (the activity) to how many victims (an output)? (e.g. number of 911 cell phones given victims)
Outcome: Are victims' lives changed? (e.g. victims report feeling safer and using 911 cell phones)

The Goal
Traditional: Meet deadlines (a compliance issue) and mass efficiency (an output ratio) (e.g. court hearing notices mailed on time to 97% of all victims)
Outcome: Victim-driven needs accomplished or remediated (e.g. victims feel less alone, are able to attend hearings)

The Focus
Traditional: Accomplish the service (an activity) (e.g. inform victims about compensation)
Outcome: Improve lives (e.g. assure victims' bills are paid)

The Accountability and Documentation
Traditional: Triggered by funder and agency requirements (e.g. compliance and activity reports)
Outcome: Motivated by victim recovery improvements (e.g. outcome measure reports)

Reporting outcomes provides valuable information about services. For example:

1. Not just what got done (outputs), but also the work accomplished for real people (outcomes)—I turned in 10 impact statements last month, and in eight of those, victims reported feeling they had a choice in participating in the justice process.

2. Not just the number of people helped (effort), but the number of victims who feel helped (results)—I helped 550 victims last year and in 80% of the returned surveys they reported feeling less alone due to my involvement.

3. Not just workload (effort), but how the work helped lighten victims' recovery loads (results)—I assisted 25 victims with compensation claims and 90% got their medical bills paid and 85% said this helped their sense of recovery.

Linking work activities with outcomes reveals Victim Advocates' progress in matching their hours completing tasks with changes in people's lives. Daily work becomes eventually recognizable as lives become safer and healthier, as rights are respected, and as debts are paid. For example, victims know their rights not just because you handed them victim rights brochures, but also because you spent time going over the brochures with them, and other staff answered their phone calls when they had more questions. Connecting the puzzle pieces is success. Success is cumulative.

> *Connecting the puzzle pieces is success. Success is cumulative.*

When is a program goal not a victim outcome goal?

Programs and grants have goals, as do most initiatives. For a goal to be a *victim* outcome goal, the result of your work must be described as a change in the victim—changed attitude, behavior, condition, knowledge, insight, status, or skill. These seven magic outcome words distinguish victim and individual outcomes from program outcomes and goals. For example, a mission statement can be a goal, as in the self-descriptions, "an agency dedicated to providing victim rights" or "an agency with caring staff who provide expert victim services." However, both are stated in output terms and neither is a victim outcome. Rather, those examples reflect efforts to do the work of providing victim rights and offering high quality (caring and expert) staff. Neither statement focuses on how the victim is improved by what they believe, do, have, know, are aware of, have become, or do better because of the victim advocacy provided to them.

Your mission is to affect change: a focus on victims' lives, not what tasks you are doing each hour. An example of a goal that is also a victim outcome is the mission statement: "To help victims prevail over the trauma of victimization by advocating and assisting for safety, healing, justice, and restitution." To help victims "prevail over the trauma of victimization" is what results from our work (it is the long-term outcome), "by advocating and assisting" is the strategy, and "safety, healing, justice, and restitution" are the outcomes and changes in victims' lives from the efforts, at least in part, of Advocates. This mission statement could also be rephrased as: "Providing assistance and advocacy that result in victims who prevail over the trauma of victimization through improved safety, healing, justice, and restitution."

Objectives are the measurable steps to reach the big picture goal. They often simply measure work done, similar to an "output." A grant objective of, "six domestic violence support groups per year" is an output objective, not an outcome, since it reports the work done. Outcome-based objectives for a support group may be that group members are able to recall and embrace three positive personal traits at moments when they experience triggers that reduce their ability to act with confidence. This objective helps victims attain the outcome goals of improved ability to make choices. Other victim outcomes could be, "I know more ways to plan for my safety," "I know more about mental and spiritual health resources." "I know more about how my case was handled," and "I have more options to try to recover financially." An objective of "twelve victims will complete the support group," is also not usually a victim outcome, since it does not describe the benefit in the lives of the graduating survivors—only that they will cross the finish line. However, it is possible for "graduating" to be a measure of a victim outcome when it is an objective for victims in the process of attaining an outcome of, for example, "self-confidence" since, it can be considered a change in status when the victim achieves a diploma. In that case the output of "graduation" is standing in for an outcome of self-sufficiency.

When are outcome or process evaluations the right tool?

Outcome evaluation involves examining the *quality of change* in victims resulting from the services provided. Outcome questions determine the success in meeting victims' needs.

Process evaluation involves examining the *service quality* of work. A process evaluation can explain how to replicate the program and can be descriptive (e.g. outlines the steps to create a satellite office or replicate the creation of a protocol). A process evaluation may ask how well a Victim Advocate and a victim interacted. Process questions are about what you do, how you do it, who receives it, how much they receive, the degree to which they are satisfied, and how the program can improve operations.

Outcome vs. Process Evaluations

Outcome evaluation is based on collected data and analyzed at the end of the program. It measures the program's impact on the victim.

Process evaluation is descriptive, explaining how the program works and how to replicate the process. It may include the program's sequences and barriers. Data is gathered and used immediately to improve the process.

Process evaluations may answer: What will we do? Did we do what we said we would do? How well did we do it (i.e. in compliance with the standards) (Edleson, 1997).

Some quality questions that are process questions include asking victims if they:

1. Found your victim service program and easily entered your building (e.g. questions about access)
2. Received the desired services (e.g. questions about structure)
3. Felt they were treated with sensitivity (e.g. questions about program process)

Other examples of process questions include: Is the program facility clean and inviting? Is the intake process user-friendly? How are staff trained? and, On what basis do staff and/or victims decide that services are no longer needed?

Asking victims if they were able to get their bills paid or if they now feel less lonely due to your services are outcome questions. Outcome evaluations also have limitations, including being unable to identify gaps in services or the need for services in different languages. It is difficult to measure what did not happen. Those gaps may become apparent from process questions and needs assessments with victims, service providers, and justice officials.

It is possible to have some overlap between process and outcome questions. Victim service programs often give help in one-time interactions when the short-term outcomes may simply be process questions about satisfaction. For example, domestic violence crisis lines often have limited opportunities to meet victim needs (an outcome issue). The victims' satisfaction (a process issue) with the sensitivity, timeliness, and accuracy of how the crisis line or rape crisis service answered their questions, provided referrals, and listened to their concerns, could be both outcome and process results.

What questions do outcomes answer?

Stakeholders are often more accustomed to output questions and measurements. However, being limited to evaluating success by counting volume of work is inadequate. Trying to establish your success by telling how many hours of counseling you provide is like claiming you deserve a Super Bowl ring based on the number of practice hours you completed. The final score of the football game is what counts. Informing a funder that a certain number of victims have received Victim Compensation is more valuable than reporting the number of applications submitted. Both types of information are important, but results trump effort. Some

Trying to establish your success by telling how many hours of counseling you provide is like claiming you deserve a Super Bowl ring based on the number of practice hours you completed.

outcome questions:

1. Donors—How will people be better off with my gift to your program?
2. Grantors—What proof is there that my investment made a difference?
3. Supervisors—How do I know staff respond to real needs of victims?
4. Educators—On what evidence are policy and program decisions based?
5. Staff—How do I know my work results in a lasting benefit?
6. Staff—Are we all working toward the same results?
7. Boards—How do we evaluate quality and usefulness of victim services?
8. Victims—Do you have a plan to meet my needs?
9. Victims—What success have you had with other victims?
10. Directors—How do I best spend money for staff, training, and services that will improve victims' lives?

Outcomes are moving targets, since no two crimes, victims, circumstances, or Victim Advocates are alike. Each situation and level of recovery has influencing factors that alter and filter needs and services. Winning the Super Bowl does not require a perfect season of winning every game, and outcome targets of victims may not all be able to be met. Perfection is the goal, but rare in this imperfect world. Still, some outcome improvements are better than none at all, and "perfect" should not be the enemy of "good." In other words, aim for perfection but accept accomplishing your best.

When the public, funders, and stakeholders ask why victim outcomes deserve priority and funding, we can point out that for a justice system to be effective in a free society, victims must call 911 and be willing to testify in order to hold law-breakers accountable. Helping victims meet their recovery needs is critical to any definition of justice. Beyond victims' pivotal role in the rule of law, society as a whole has a special moral obligation to those citizens whom family, neighbors, and safety services could not protect. Victims of crime deserve our best efforts, for "there but for the grace of God go I."

Some other ways to understand outcome measures:

1. Victim-driven services resulting in heart-warming stories of lives changed (e.g. using anecdotes of how victims being and feeling excluded from hearings changed into empowered and self-confident participants with meaningful roles in the system)
2. The impact of expert victim advocacy on victims' problems (e.g.

> *Outcomes are moving targets, since no two crimes, victims, circumstances, or Victim Advocates are alike.*

using collaborations to provide emotional recovery through children's play therapy, attachment security with transitional pet care, child custody through legal assistance, and financial stability with permanent housing advocacy)

3. The framework of victim comments, e.g.:

   a. "If it weren't for you, I don't know where I'd be. You saved my life." (Safety)

   b. "You gave me hope and helped give me choices." (Healing)

   c. "You helped me get him prosecuted." (Justice)

   d. "You helped me get my bills paid." (Restitution)

Chapter 2 Summary: Understanding Outcomes

To attain value for stakeholders and success for victims, the "come home to mama" summary is that four victim-oriented quality areas work seamlessly to meet victim-driven needs for safety, healing, justice, and restitution (i.e. financial recovery). Victims are thus improved in their attitudes or values, behaviors, conditions, knowledge, insights, status, or skills.

The core reason victim advocacy programs exist is to help victims improve their lives. But how do we really know when lives are changing? It is not how hard we are working; it is whether victims are recovering. These changes in victims' lives are outcomes. Services measured and evaluated by, for example, quantity, proper sequence, and timeliness are process measures. Evaluating our work culture and understanding of success on the differences our services make in each victim reached are outcome measures. Program goals, descriptions, and implementation must be centered on how victims access, receive, are treated, and benefit from our services. A perfectly operated hospital that does not result in patient healing is not successful, and likewise our task is to focus on the outcomes of our work in the lives of victims.

Answers for the Pop Quiz - Understanding Outcomes:

1. <u>c</u> How a program flows from beginning to end, with such things as job titles and tasks labeled along the flow, are items in a process evaluation.

2. <u>a</u> Performance-based measures include both outcome <u>and output</u> goals and levels used in finance, manufacturing, and the federal government to focus on stakeholder results.

3. <u>d</u> Victims having choices, increasing their sense of empowerment, and improving their safety are all outcome goals appropriate to victim advocacy.

4. <u>b</u> Providing victim rights, as well as accurate and timely restitution reports, reflect wonderful attitudes and actions of Victim Advocates, however they are program goals, and are NOT victim outcomes.

Chapter 3
The Outcome Logic Model
The Picture of Program Purpose

What is a logic model?

A logic model is a word picture of the purpose, content, and sequence of your program. The task of a logic model is to portray how a program is supposed to work theoretically, with all its parts linked, and how to improve its results (outcomes) by adjusting its components. It is the *logical* description of the program's correlating parts. It depicts assumed causal connection, not cause-effect relationships. It reflects your working assumptions and not (necessarily) research findings or all the influencing factors to reach your outcome goals. It is the foundation for program planning and evaluation (Welcome to Enhancing Program Performance with Logic Models, 2002).

Logic models can be diagrams, flow charts, or other visual depictions that link the reasoning of "what causes what" in accomplishing the goal. Logic models often have a few common parts—inputs, activities, outputs, and outcomes—and then each program ascribes its unique situation into the model. In other words, your program will fill in the blanks for which inputs, activities, outputs, and outcomes are unique to the victims your program seeks to serve (Innovation Network, 2005).

Your logic model is your theory of change; how you predict your program will accomplish improvements in your clients (e.g. hospital patients, rehabilitation clients, crime victims). The logic model can provide as simple or as complex an overview of how the organization works as its designer intends to demonstrate. The logic model is a guide. It describes, "the way we do things around here" from your problem to your solution. It is your *modus operandi*. It is not an action plan, but rather a convincing strategy on why you do what you do. For example, when a staff member questions if he or she should perform a particular victim service, the answer is to point to where on the model that service is linked to reaching an outcome. A good logic model is worth a thousand words because it communicates your story with a handful of words, images, and concepts of how you link the problem needing fixed with the work you do and the

> *The logic model is a guide. It describes, "the way we do things around here" from your problem to your solution.*

change your work accomplishes in people's lives. It helps you move from being just a service delivery organization to a learning organization that can adapt services for individual victims and for similar groups of victims.

The advantage of more complex models is the increased ability to test and measure each program component to determine how and what to adjust in order to affect the mission of the program. For example, the intended adjustment can be to improve a service process that will affect the life of a victim (the outcome). The disadvantage of more complex models is the difficulty and expense of tracking and linking multiple services all interconnected with resources (inputs), influencing factors, and outputs, while also measuring or estimating the percentage impact of a particular outcome. The more information, the more staff expenses for analysis and reporting. Below is a simple model and its flow from your planned work (inputs and activities) to your intended results (outputs and outcomes).

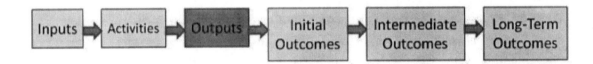

The further out from the outputs a program seeks to attain an outcome, the less influence the program has. The number and degree of influencing factors also limits the program's ability to impact longer-term outcomes. For example, explaining victim rights information (an activity) will hopefully result in victims (number of victims is the output) having increased knowledge (an initial outcome). Providing court advocacy (an activity) may or may not ensure a victim's right to be heard (an outcome of improved status). If a judge decides to restrict the victim from presenting a victim impact statement, this influencing factor would tend to produce an undesirable outcome for the victim. However, even adverse outcomes are a source of learning for program staff. Data about worsened outcomes can be collected and used to educate and influence policies and court decisions for future victims wanting to provide a victim impact statement.

What are the main parts of a logic model?

An input is what is required to do the work of the program. Inputs are the investment in, and foundation for the program. They also reflect the parameters of the program. Inputs are nouns. They include the resources and materials consumed and needed in the program's activities and structure that are required for the program to exist and function. Some

Some inputs are:

• Money

• Volunteers

• Victims Rights Laws

• Materials

• Resources

• Staff

• Equipment

• Facilities

• Court Rulings

input examples:

1. Organizational—Funding, facilities, equipment, supplies, volunteers, staff, materials, time
2. Environmental—Court rules, laws, funding restrictions, contract terms, technology limitations, partners, research base

An activity is an action, service, task, or process. It tells what work is accomplished. Some examples:

1. Program—Providing services, such as, assisting with victim impact statements, engaging in crisis counseling, sheltering victims, facilitating support groups, filing protection orders
2. Administrative—training staff, coordinating meetings, recruiting volunteers, working with the media, analyzing survey responses, writing grants, engaging in policy advocacy

An output is a number; the units of service for the program. It reflects your workload and totals the data of what is done (the activities). It summarizes how much assistance (services & programs) you are providing, and to what type and how many victims in a specific time (e.g. number of support groups held quarterly, number of victims assisted annually, number of hours of service provided daily, and number of court notices sent monthly). They are ingredients needed to attain victim desired outcomes.

A victim outcome is a change in the victims' well-being. It is the impact of services in victims' lives. An outcome is a target; where victim needs intersect with program services. It is the basis for why we do what we do. The effect or impact of victim advocacy is the outcome. Negative results are outcomes also. We prefer positive outcomes, but we can learn from negative outcomes as well. If we do this work (activities), then the victims will have changed attitudes, behaviors, conditions, knowledge, insights, status, or skills. As noted earlier, an outcome is reached (partially or wholly) when victims are impacted in what they believe, do, have, know, are aware of, have become, or do better (e.g. they feel safer, bills are paid). Outcomes are goals within varying degrees of the program's control or influence. A short-hand method to remember the essential outcomes is the acronym: ABC KISS. [See sidebar]

However, for planning purposes and developing logic models, ABC KISS is not the general sequence of accomplishing outcomes. The flow of personal/victim change is most likely:

1. Improved Condition (or Alleviated Crisis)
2. New Knowledge
3. Enhanced Insight
4. Changed Attitude
5. Increased Skill

Some activities are:
- Writing victim impact statements
- Providing crisis counseling
- Filing protection orders

Some outputs are:
- Units of service provided
- Volume of work accomplished

Victim outcomes are:
- Changed Attitudes
- Modified Behaviors
- Improved Conditions
- New Knowledge
- Enhanced Insights
- Altered Status
- Increased Skills

Attitude

Behavior

Condition

Knowledge

Insight

Status

Skill

6. Modified Behavior

7. Altered Status

What are the three levels of outcomes?

The three time dimensions of outcomes are initial, intermediate, and long-term, with each level potentially sub-divided into tiers. The time frames are features of the program design and are not set. For example, one victim-counseling program might consider long-term outcomes as results from six months of weekly sessions, while another counseling program might consider long-term outcomes as being five-year results.

Initial (immediate, early, or short-term) outcomes might include knowledge, insights, skills, opinions, attitudes, awareness, and motivation. For example, did the knowledge of the victims increase as demonstrated by their increased awareness, understanding, and/or problem solving ability? Did the victims' attitudes improve in their changed outlooks, viewpoints, or perspectives? Did victims' skills improve as reflected in their increased verbal or physical abilities and/or new performance levels? Again, the time frame of initial outcomes is relative and not predictable. Victims with a need for change may present both initial outcomes that must be met within hours as well as needs that may require six weeks of crisis intervention.

Intermediate (middle, 2nd stage, or medium) outcomes often include behaviors, practices, and decision-making. For example, did the observable actions or reactions of victims improve when in stressful situations? Did victims make self-empowering choices and/or safety enhancing preparations to deal with potential or actual violent situations? When possible, measuring behaviors, choices, or other outcomes should include some pre-test or self-analysis (or other) comparison to a baseline in determining the level of improvement or change.

Long-term (ultimate, eventual, longer time-frame) outcomes are down-the-road changes commonly in values, beliefs, and status, such as the victim's social, economic, safety, justice, and environmental situation.

These concepts fit together in a visual pattern or model. One of the most common outcome models is the United Way Outcome Logic Model (Hatry, Houten, Plantz, Taylor Greenway, 1996).

Inputs are the foundation for the program. Inputs can be the parameters of the program, such as jurisdiction or legal limits, but primarily include the administrative and organizational content of a program. Programs use the inputs to do the work, services, and activities benefiting the victims. That work is reflected in the output numbers of what was done, who was reached, and in what time period it was completed. The activities measured and described by degree and amount in the outputs, result in outcomes and life

In Arizona, to help illustrate this outcome progression for local Victims Of Crime Act (VOCA) sub-grantees, the former state VOCA administrator, Roger Illingworth, characterized the progress of victims (Illingworth, 2002) as:

Long-term—what victims realize and experience (e.g. experience less crime-related symptoms, better support system, feel a greater sense of control, feel safer because of services)

Intermediate—what victims engage in, act upon, or participate in (e.g. use coping skills, better able to access needed services, participate in and have choices in the criminal justice system)

Initial—what new knowledge victims have (e.g. more knowledgeable about victim services, better understanding of crisis and trauma, more knowledgeable about victim/legal rights)

changes for victims (Valley of the Sun, 2008). Program activities (e.g. tasks, job duties) are designed and linked to attaining victim needs and outcomes. Outcomes are the victim goals that begin with the initial outcomes first, the crisis or preliminary needs of victims. Initial outcomes are important to victims since they are the foundation for attaining the second level of outcomes, the intermediate and ongoing needs. Intermediate outcomes are critical steps for victims to prevail over their individual victimization problems in order to reach their personal long-term outcomes (e.g. ultimate safety, emotional and spiritual healing, offender accountability and a sense of justice, and/or financial recovery and stability goals).

How do services and quality fit into a logic model?

The activities and services the program provides fall under an outcome area. For example, the safety outcome has services of protection order assistance and safety planning, and the emotional healing outcome has counseling and a 24 hour crisis line.

The big picture of victim advocacy recognizes that the variety of crimes, influencing factors, and victim experiences seem infinite and difficult to organize. However, the relatively common needs of safety, physical and psychological recovery, fairness and justice, and financial recovery and stability remain the nucleus. In designing a plan to meet those needs, the access, structure, and process components are useful guides to quality. Another stable guide is recognizing that victims must start with addressing their early and emergency needs first, and that, hopefully, most victims will progress in their recovery, changing their needs over time.

As victims vary greatly, so also do their needs. Each outcome is further broken down into needs that are more distinct. Programs cannot address all victims' needs. Their missions must be narrowed and the partnerships expanded to accomplish the best results for the most (or specific) victims that the available inputs (resources) allow.

A clear mission and a logical program design are valuable to help victims understand their situations and possible options for recovery. They also help counter Murphy's Law, that if something can go wrong, it will. They help organize the natural tendency of organizations to creep or drift into routines that may not be helpful in improving victims' lives. If you wish you had a photograph or diagram of a program's mission and services, then you want an outcome logic model: an image of what most victims need in the most common sequence. Victim outcome logic models can be understood generically like concepts and stages of how people recovery from grief. Similarly, victim outcome models are not prescriptive or absolute for any particular victim.

Many Victims, Many Different Needs

Program Quality: access; structure and process; reaching, assisting, and respecting victims

Mission Quality: victim safety, healing, justice, and restitution; improving victims' lives

Many Victims, Many Different Outcomes

- Not all victims need all outcomes of safety, healing, justice, and restitution

- No two victims recover exactly alike

Many Victims, Many Common Experiences

Common experiences necessitate a Victim Outcome Logic Model, which includes a word-picture of your services, a diagram of how victims will recover, and a sequence of service options.

How do you read a logic model from the bottom to the top?

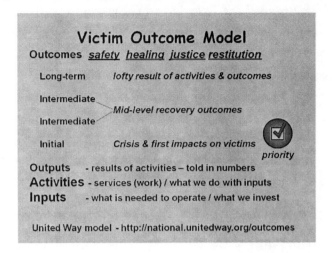

You can visualize the outcome logic model as a pyramid with early critical needs addressed as the bottom layer. Over time, longer-term needs become the focus as victims progress toward the peak of the pyramid composed of the four primary needs. Individual victim recovery is usually progressive, but may not be orderly, linear, or spiraled. The outcome model is instructive and not rigid. It is based on working assumptions of the logic of cause and effect, and consequently must be constantly informed by research on such linkages and the roles of influencing factors.

For some victims, the initial outcome may be a goal needing to be addressed within the first hour. The advocacy response might be reducing their trauma with crisis counseling, improving their condition with emergency money to pay for medicine, or providing safe shelter. It is common sense to address crisis issues first, since, for example, explaining the details of the victims' compensation program to most victims during the first phase of their victimization is not likely to promote healing when they are still focusing on their suddenly chaotic and unsafe world. Helping victims know they are not alone is an initial outcome for some victims, and it establishes a foundation for interaction for future advocacy. Long-term outcomes are the overarching life adjustment issues resulting from the crime.

In other words, the earliest and most important needs that victim advocacy must meet and measure are initial outcomes. After the initial outcomes, the intermediate (or midway) outcomes lead to reaching long-term outcomes at the top of the model. The priority is always to address initial outcomes first because they are the ones that come first in victim's lives, and because programs have the most influence in helping attain them.

Ideally, services are available to victims immediately after the victimization, and continue as long as needed. Obviously, program

The earliest and most important needs that victim advocacy must meet and measure are initial outcomes.

limitations (e.g. funding, jurisdiction, and staffing levels) will require prioritization of victims and services. A realistic option is to maximize partner collaborations (e.g. protocols, mergers, overlap reduction) to meet the most victim outcomes for the most victims. Still, administrators confront choices between victims to be served and services to provide. For example, is it a higher priority to serve all victims reporting a violent crime with triage advocacy such as family contacts, death notification, safety review, medical treatment assistance, justice process orientation, crisis counseling, and victim compensation information, or to assist fewer victims with more specific, clinical, in-depth, and expert court advocacy services?

For most victims, their needs will change as their recovery processes and life circumstances shift, and new needs will emerge. It is common sense to deal with first things first (initial outcomes first) and more complex problems later. Multiple outcomes in the logic model's initial and intermediate sections help guide victim service staff on the generic road to recovery, and remind Victim Advocates that there are other issues to consider with victims besides their obvious presenting problems.

> *For most victims, their needs will change as their recovery processes and life circumstances shift, and new needs will emerge.*

How does reading the model up and down connect with reading it side to side?

Viewing each outcome box on the chart horizontally represents the "what else is needed" by victims before moving upward to other outcomes. Any outcome along the row needed by the victim at that stage and not met could hinder the ability to reach future improvements.

The chart can also be viewed vertically, starting at the bottom by noting the "if-then" connection to the outcomes above. *If* the victim attains the lower outcome, *then* the next outcome above is more likely to be met, and so on up the chart to the long-term outcome. Starting at the bottom, outcomes also answers the question, "Why?" The reason to address initial outcomes is that each is valuable for the victim, and each is linked to the next steps of outcomes. Helping victims past their crisis stages helps them move to more complex or higher outcomes. The reverse also is possible. Starting at the top with the long-term outcome, the question, "How?" is answered by going down from any point in the chart. The question, "How did you help this victim attain this long-term outcome?" is answered by pointing out the prior outcomes that the victim was assisted with first. The logic of these connections and incremental steps is why it is called a logic model.

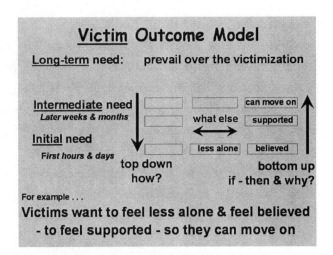

When beginning a model do you start from the top or the bottom?

There is no right answer for where to start building a model. Many program developers start from the top of the outcome model, determining the long-term outcomes first. This requires flexibility. For example, if a grant or supervisor only assigns a general direction and not specific outcomes, you probably want to start at the top. The big picture questions require answers to what the overall purpose of the program is, what difference the program will make in victims' lives, and what success will look like (defining success).

If you have no choice on the outcome goals, and they are either absolute from grantors or are sacred cows that must be accepted as goals for one reason or another, then start from the bottom asking, "What does it take to reach that outcome?" You also start from the bottom when you are validating an existing program and have little flexibility in changing activities or services.

Both starting points have distinct benefits when beginning to design an outcome model. In any case, reading a logic model from the bottom up answers the question, "Why are we doing this?" The answer is to make an early life improvement in order to then accomplish the next tier or level of outcomes. Evaluating an outcome model from the top down answers the question, "How do we accomplish this?" The answer is by first attaining the prior level or tier of outcomes below in the model to help the victim move farther in the recovery process. The key is to assure the logical linkage between each outcome in the model as either a precursor to the one above or a successor of the outcome below.

Reading a logic model from the bottom up answers the question, "Why are we doing this?"

How long range should outcomes be in the model?

Outcomes should be close enough to be attained, influenced, challenging, and meaningful. The long-range outcomes do not have to be under the control of the program to be meaningful (Plantz, Taylor Greenway, Hendricks, 2008). Meaningful is defined as having value for victims. Outcomes must capture what your organization is about, including immediate concerns as well as the goals victims have down the road. Victim outcomes' theoretical links to each other and with linked activities of victim advocates and partners must be plausible; that is, informed by research and/or the victims and stakeholders involved with attaining the logic model outcomes.

If the program is complex, it is appropriate to create multiple models that are linked to each other. A macro-model could include related outcome logic models with community, state or national parent programs or parallel programs within an agency. Likewise, a micro-model could take a domestic violence or sexual assault outcome of helping victims to not feel alone and a create sub-model for peer support group outcomes, and a peer support group could have sub-logic models to focus on how to reach and meet the needs of particular gender, language, or ethnic populations in a peer support group.

A good test of any model is to carefully consider if each outcome is foundational to attaining the next outcome above, and in reverse, if each outcome is directly (at least partially) a result from accomplishing the outcome(s) below. When in doubt, brainstorm with victims and professionals regarding their experience on what pattern of improvements might be linked with each other. For example, when wondering how some victims reach a significantly higher level of self-confidence and empowerment, and knowing this does not happen by magic, consider what incremental steps (outcomes) might explain how victims attained such improvements.

Programs have less influence over future goals than immediate ones, but services can assist victims in attaining future goals nonetheless. Designing services to help victims attain future goals is critical to understanding the larger map of the forest while journeying among the barrier trees of the moment. For example, a victim's difficulties paying rent and utility bills are less likely if the emergency medicine and food needs are taken care of promptly. The emergency needs will remain a priority until resolved to the satisfaction of the victim.

The priority for most victim service programs are initial outcomes. Early needs often include emergency security, personal support for trauma, law enforcement contact and investigation, medical examination and

Pop Quiz: Outcome Model

1. 15 victims attend the weekly support group

2. 85% of victims report reduced nightmares

3. The victim's emergency medical bill is paid

4. Staff are nationally credentialed

5. Victim Advocates are giving out cell phones

6. A victim no longer feels the trauma of a crime

Choose the correct program issue for each action.

1. _____

2. _____

3. _____

4. _____

5. _____

6. _____

a. Input

b. Activity

c. Output

d. Initial outcome

e. Intermediate outcome

f. Long-term outcome

Answers for the Pop Quiz - Outcome Model:

1. Output

2. Intermediate outcome

3. Initial outcome

4. Input

5. Activity

6. Long-term outcome

treatment, prescriptions, transportation, shelter, and food. Getting past initial needs will likely allow victims to consider participating in later services, such as clinical or peer support groups and transitional housing. After addressing the intermediate needs, the victim can address long-term life adjustment issues resulting from the crime. Each step of recovery lays the groundwork for the next phase of possible recovery issues.

The success of services in reaching early outcomes are not only easier to measure, but also are tied more directly to program services (and partnerships).

The success of services in reaching early outcomes are not only easier to measure, but also are tied more directly to program services (and partnerships). Measuring intermediate and long-term outcomes often requires significant research expertise and staff time to try to determine the impact staff activities had on complex human emotional and behavioral conditions. With the initial outcomes, doing the right work well is more likely to result in positive outcomes.

The outcome model is simply a guide to know what to try when, and what issues are most likely to be considered next with victims. For example, a program may only be able to have an 85% influence on any initial outcome (e.g. know more about victim rights), and only a 15% impact on reaching a long-term outcome (e.g. have a positive experience with justice system).

Can appropriate activities result in negative outcomes?

It is possible for "correct" program activities to result in a negative outcome. For example, to help victims feel safer you might provide more information about the offender, such as the details of the crime, theories on the motives, and the progress of the investigation. Yet, for some victims knowing all this could actually make them more fearful. Some criminals are dangerous and some investigations make no progress. On the other hand, the victim's informed fear of a dangerous criminal may help keep them vigilant and help them know what precautions to take which might keep them alive (which is a positive outcome). In any case, we want to know the likely effects of our services since the point of measuring is to figure out how we can improve lives.

Positive outcomes do not automatically result when programs implement a tested outcome methodology or a researched set of activities. There is no exact cause and effect relationship between program activities and improvements in victims' outcomes. Programs cannot guarantee any service will meet a victim's need. Victim choice, among other factors, is a primary variable. Victim services provide notice, information, crisis counseling, and short-term shelter, but services can not make a victim safe, ensure future trust in people again, automatically produce a sense of justice, or (usually) make sure that all crime-related bills are paid.

Giving important information multiple times verbally and in writing does not guarantee that victims will remember or learn the information. Assisting a victim with documenting restitution and receiving a court order for restitution, or helping a victim file for insurance and compensation does not ensure that the offender will pay or that insurance or the state victim's compensation program will grant the claim amount. Rather, the effort to help the victim could simply add to the victim's lost work time, frustration, and feeling of violation.

Outcome results, regardless if measured as positive or negative, need to be evaluated. Hopefully the measuring is being done for the right reasons and we can trust that the results will not be used against us in situations we can not control. Considerations include whether the outcome indicator is accurate for the outcome, and if the program directly influenced the outcomes. One method that helps in this inquiry is to review what influencing factors exist, and then assign estimated percentages to each one as to its importance in the outcome measure. Is it possible that the service's influence in attaining the outcome is weak? Is the influence increasing or declining, and upon what basis is the conclusion reached?

What is the difference between Victim and Program outcomes?

Victim outcomes are changes in victims. Program outcomes are performance measures of quality issues, such as access, structure, process, satisfaction (i.e. victim reflections on efforts to assist them), efficiency, and can include improvements in victims' lives. All the inputs, activities, and outputs (quality issues) help produce victim outcomes, and all the victims' outcomes rolled together are the program results, outcomes. The danger in discussing victim outcomes in the same breath as program outcomes is that, without research results, no causality link can be reported. Measurements are indicators that we might be heading the right direction, but only carefully constructed research designs can attribute victim changes to a program intervention—and even then, multiple research replications are needed to increase our sense of confidence for any link between a program activity and a victim outcome. A second caution is that high quality does not necessarily result in improved victim outcomes, just as perfectly followed medical protocols do not always link to improved patient health.

The danger in discussing victim outcomes in the same breath as program outcomes is that, without research results, no causality link can be reported.

There are distinctions between measuring victim and program changes. The steps to achieve a program goal can be designed with the help of logic models, for example, for resource development, organizational planning, public education, and volunteer recruitment (Nnanabu, 2006) [See Exhibits 2a and 2b for examples of program logic models] (CDC-RPE Logic Model, 2007). Program logic models should link toward a victim outcome since

Victim Outcome—the degree to which a victim need is met or ameliorated. It is a measure of personal change. For example, a victim feels less alone or has bills paid after receiving a victim advocacy assisted restitution payment.

Program Effectiveness—the degree to which a service or organizational goal is met (the mission is accomplished). It is usually a measure of effort. However, the service measures can combine with the victim outcomes to be, in total, the program effectiveness. For example, if your efforts are successful in improving forensic medical rape exams, then your program has been effective in measureable improvements in timeliness (e.g. the exam time is cut by three hours), accuracy (e.g. the evidence collected is useful 50% more frequently for investigations), and cultural sensitivity (e.g. 98% of Limited English Proficiency victims have an appropriate interpreter). Victims reporting feeling believed and aware of their medical choices during the hospital exam stage are examples of victim outcomes and are added measures of program effectiveness.

Listening to victims is the logical home base for designing and implementing an outcome model.

ultimately they are directed toward improving the likelihood that victims will prevail over the trauma of their victimization. An example of a program goal is, "increased community involvement in victim advocacy," with the objectives of, for example, increasing donations for children to have age appropriate toys, participation of community volunteers for childcare and transportation of victims, and civic club donations for emergency needs of victims. Another program model possibility is, "non-victim witness preparation," to increase public participation in providing evidence. The theoretical link to a victim outcome is that this program will lead to more information in the justice process, which leads to increased reliability of evidence, which leads to offender accountability, and thus, may lead to an increased sense of justice and more case knowledge and insight for victims.

How do you start linking the model parts?

As noted earlier, there is no right way to create and link a logic model diagram. One suggestion is to start by using the chart below, working from the right side (McNamara, 1997-2006):

1. Determine what the outcomes are that victims desire and that your program (and limitations) appear to be able to influence
2. Determine the activities and services that are most likely to attain those outcomes, including how to perform them (their design, depth, timing, sequence, etc.)
3. Determine the output level necessary for the activities to make the difference needed to attain the outcome (how many, how often, numbers of staff, etc.)
4. Determine the inputs (resources) needed to perform the activities at the planned output level

Remember, there is a balance between meeting each victim in their unique situation, and knowing when other victims' experiences may be instructive for use with that victim. Similar sounding victimizations are a guide to meeting needs, yet can lead Victim Advocates to the common error of presuming those similarities automatically link to certain services. Advocates must listen from the heart, remembering that the environment and culture of each victim's story affects his or her needs and outcomes within the broad categories of safety, healing, justice, and financial recovery (Victim Satisfaction, 2006).

Determining specific victim needs, and significant influencing factors is key to creating an outcome model that will stand the test of time, recognizing that all the while influencing factors like technology and culture are changing. Listening to victims is the logical home base for designing and implementing an outcome model.

Victim Outcome Model Sequence

INPUTS	ACTIVITIES	OUTPUTS	OUTCOMES
Resources dedicated to or consumed by the program	What the program does with the inputs to fulfill its mission to improve victims	The products from the program	The result of products & activities is change in victims' lives
What are the resources you need?	What is the work you will do?	What is the amount and time frame in which you will do the work?	How will the victim situation be different?
# 4 – fourth	# 2 – second	# 3 – third	# 1 – Start here: what the victim needs

When do you use theory, outcome, and activity logic models?

Since a logic model is a graphic mirror of your thinking, as your questions vary you can adapt the logic model concept to your changing need. For example, describing your theory and strategy of how change will happen is different than illustrating how you will evaluate or implement the program. The W.K. Kellogg Foundation (W.K. Kellogg Foundation Logic Model Development Guide, 2004), explains three different approaches to logic models:

1. "Theory Approach Models emphasize the theory of change that has influenced the design and plan for the program." These models explain the assumptions and reasons for a program, and may include the problem or issue addressed and the reasons certain types of solution strategies and related activities are selected. They explain how and why your program will work and reflect "big picture" concepts of your program. They may be helpful in making your case in a grant proposal (W.K. Kellogg, 2004, p. 9).

2. "Outcomes Approach Models focus on the early aspects of program planning and attempt to connect the resources and/or activities with the desired results in a workable program." These models "outline the approach and expectations behind a program's intended results" and are "useful in designing effective evaluation and reporting strategies" (W.K. Kellogg, 2004, p. 10).

3. "Activities Approach Model pays the most attention to the specifics of the implementation process. A logic model of this type links the various planned activities together in a manner that maps the process of program implementation. These models describe what a program intends to do and as such are most useful for the purpose

of program monitoring and management. This type provides the detailed steps you think you will need to follow to implement your program" (W.K. Kellogg, 2004, p. 10).

Your choice of logic model can change not only how and why you approach your program, but also when you seek to create a logic model during the life of your program. The W.K. Kellogg Foundation suggests a different logic model template for Program Planning (for clarifying program theory), Program Implementation (for demonstrating your program's progress), and Program Evaluation (for program evaluation questions and indicators) (W.K. Kellogg, 2004, pgs.14, 54, 57, 59, 61).

Chapter 3 Summary: The Outcome Logic Model

The classic outcome logic model has inputs (your resources and parameters), activities (your work and effort), and outputs (your count of quantity and frequency of work) as the foundation for the outcomes (your work results measured in improved lives of victims). The key outcomes of change in people are found in the letters ABC KISS: Attitude, Behavior, Condition, Knowledge, Insight, Status, and Skill. The improvement in the lives of victims usually arrives in stages, with initial outcomes reached in the first few minutes, hours, or days. Next are the intermediate changes in coming weeks and months, with the long-term outcomes often being lifetime goals or years in the making. That progression can be diagramed for individuals and groups of victims to show how inputs, activities, outputs, and the outcome progression are linked. This book is focused on outcomes of victims, that is, meeting their safety, healing, justice, and financial restitution needs, and not on program outcomes. Program outcomes can similarly link inputs, activities, outputs, and outcomes to reflect how organizational goals are achieved (or why they might fail) and how the community is impacted. Logic models can be adapted depending on whether you want to explain your theory of change (why you designed your program the way you did), your outcome achievement plan (how you link your work with outcome improvements), and/or your activity progression (how you systematically implement and manage your program).

Outcomes Represent a Cultural Change

If outcomes are part of Victim Advocates' daily conversations and definitions of success, then our culture has changed, while our passion for quality never stops.

Chapter 4
A Victim Outcome Logic Model
Designing for universal and unique victim needs

What are the core victim needs?

Four basic areas of need affect victims of crime—safety, healing, justice, and restitution (financial recovery).

Core Victim Needs

actual & perceived	spiritual emotional & medical	fairness & system treatment	resources & financial stability
SAFETY	HEALING	JUSTICE	RESTITUTION

Most victim needs fit into these four categories. However, not all victims have all four needs or have these needs at the same time or in the same sequence. Even victims in unsolved crimes, such as arson or burglary, may need advocacy with investigators, payment of crime-related bills, crisis counseling, or emergency shelter. The federal government's Victims of Crime Act (VOCA) Guidelines from 1995 and 1997 reference four similar categories. The 1997 VOCA version reads, "For the purpose of these Program Guidelines, direct services are defined as those efforts that (1) respond to the emotional and physical needs of crime victims; (2) assist primary and secondary victims of crime to stabilize their lives after a victimization; (3) assist victims to understand and participate in the criminal justice system; and (4) provide victims of crime with a measure of safety, such as boarding-up broken windows and replacing or repairing locks" (U.S. Department of Justice, 1997, p. 7). These are similar to the outcomes of healing (emotional and physical needs), restitution/financial stability (stabilize their lives), justice (understand and participate in the criminal justice process), and safety (measure of safety).

Every victim is different, and some may not care about each outcome of safety, healing, justice, or restitution. A victim may, for example, prioritize privacy as the healing outcome he or she seeks or a civil justice remedy

Not all victims have all four needs or have these needs at the same time or in the same sequence.

Sample Victim Model Diagram Templates (Taylor-Powell, 2005)

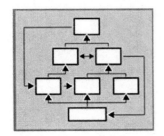

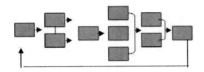

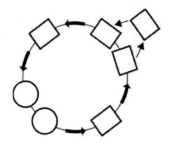

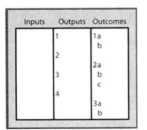

as the justice outcome (Victim Rights Law Center, 2008). Most victims, however, describe their experience with common feelings and problems (Lowenstein, 2000). Like a marriage counselor adapting to different clients, there remains a foundation of common issues and strategies. These four outcomes are the broad needs of victims from which some common and many individual outcomes branch (Zweig & Burt, 2007, p. 1149).

What does a general victim outcome model look like?

There is no single correct design for a victim outcome logic model. A preferred model by many grantors and managers is one that links graphic boxes of initial, intermediate, and long-term outcomes with arrows reflecting the linkage and progression of outcomes. The visual imagery should be concise so observers can quickly grasp the logical correlations and the identifiable changes in lives. Logic models can be formatted to flow vertically, horizontally, or circularly, as well as a map, diagram or other pattern.

On the following page is a sample comprehensive (master plan) victim outcome logic model design, which includes the four components of safety, healing, justice, and restitution.

What are the primary outcomes for Safety?

There is no greater victim need than safety. A life-threatening and life-changing experience due to an offender violating and controlling a person undermines trust in normal relationships. Routines can seem overwhelming in situations that otherwise appear safe or reasonable. Fears of new attacks can continue while waiting or progressing through the justice, healing, and financial recovery processes. Assisting victims with immediate security concerns is the highest priority (Young, Davis, Lurigio, & Herman, 2007), recognizing that there are different meanings of that concept between victims, victim service staff, justice officials, and the community (Curran, 2008).

Safety services through victim advocacy can include everything from assisting in finding safe shelter or protective custody, and providing emergency 911 cell phones. It can also include addressing emergency security issues (doors, windows, locks, security systems, etc.), assisting with protection orders, and working with law enforcement. Furthermore, Advocates can aid victim support personnel, coworkers, and neighbors in safety planning. Individual and family safety plans are particularly beneficial when practiced or role-played with children at a level most appropriate for their age.

Some victims do not want to leave their abusers; they just want the violence to stop. This calls for individualized and ever-changing safety planning to find the balance between supporting victim safety, changing the culture of

Victim Outcome Model (Master Plan)

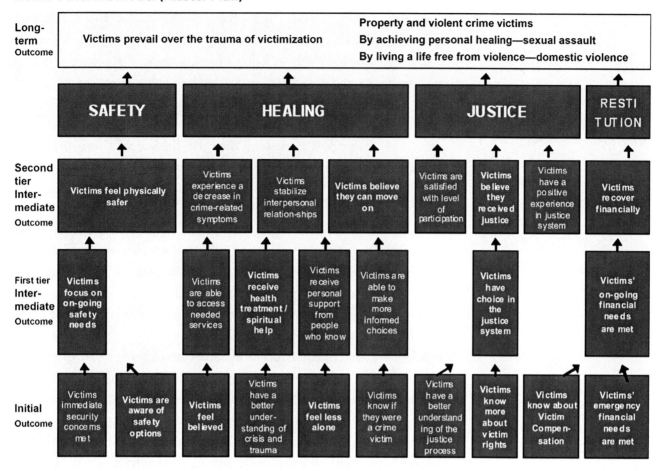

Outcome Model for Safety

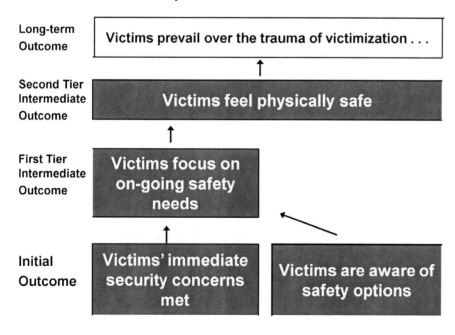

There are some critical initial needs of victims: to know if they were crime victims; to begin to comprehend what they are going through; and, to feel believed and less alone.

the relationship, and ending the violent behaviors of the abuser.

Providing safety information, options, and direct assistance are the critical initial needs to meet. This process includes developing safety plans with victims and assisting them in being more aware of community resources. The informative and non-directive attitudes of Victim Advocates are key factors in encouraging victims to return for assistance in the future. Victims need to know that support is available to them for as long as it is necessary to understand, accept, and accomplish their self-directed safety outcomes. [For sample activities and outputs for safety outcomes, see Exhibit 4a]

What are the primary outcomes for Healing?

Victimization affects people's emotional, spiritual (Lord, J.H., 2006), and physical well being. In this complexity, there are some critical initial needs of victims: to know if they were crime victims; to begin to comprehend what they are going through; and, to feel believed and less alone. Integrated into these initial core areas is the victims accepting that the crimes were not their fault, and that the responsibility and culpability lies with the offenders. Intermediate needs include victims being aware of and able to access safety and community resources, strengthening support teams, and receiving spiritual and long-term health treatment (Mental Health Response to Mass Violence and Terrorism, 2005).

Determining if an experience truly is a crime can be the first hurdle. If a robber holds a gun to a bank teller's head, there is no doubt the victim is

Outcome Model for Healing

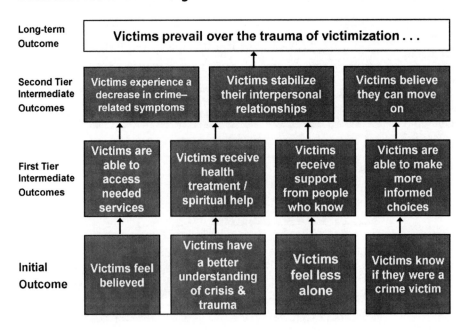

the bank teller. For other victims, the situation may be less clear. Sometimes victims of sexual assault present to rape crisis hotlines or centers not knowing if what they have experienced was criminal. In addition, people may awaken from anesthesia feeling something is wrong. Maybe dim memories will force them to question whether they were victims of assault while drunk, asleep, or drugged. Some individuals have family physical relationships and interactions that they have come to believe are normal, thus they question the legal definition of sexual assault. Others are so naïve that they do not even know that what was done to them was criminal assault, or they are too embarrassed to talk about it. Victim advocates need to be cautious and comforting when helping individuals process these types of situations.

Whether or not a crime took place is sometimes called into question by victims of a variety of crimes. A home burns—is it arson? An ex-boyfriend causes fear when demonstrating unwanted affection and threatens suicide if rejected—is it stalking? A credit card bill appears with multiple, mysterious charges or with unrecognized company names—is it identity theft? Multiple employees find health insurance bills unpaid—is it a human resource department error or a theft of employee paid premiums? Careful listening and exploring of concerns with law enforcement investigators are usually the best responses for Victim Advocates in addressing such crime victims' concerns.

The victims' circles of family, friends, and other support persons are often the key components in facing their new future.

The victims' circles of family, friends, and other support persons are often the key components in facing their new future. Emotional healing may result from expert victim services. However, the role of Victim Advocates is to include, with the victims' consent and guidance, the victims' trusted support systems, for long-term recovery. Victims should be encouraged to share the facts of the crime as well as the emotions evoked by the crime, as much and as often as they feel comfortable. They can be reminded that it is their choice how and when to tell others; recognizing that they cannot control how loved ones will react or whom else might be told (Santa Barbara Rape Crisis Center, 2000).

Helping victims understand their crises and traumas can include examining their level of personal violation, whether it is a theft, robbery, assault, sexual assault, or homicide. Each victim has unique experiences of intensity, loss of control, violation of trust, as well as a decline in health (e.g. depression) and other effects. For some victims it is helpful to understand why they reacted with the normal emotional or physical trauma responses of fight, flight, collapse, freeze, numbness, etc. Often their particular response relates to prior life experiences. Gender, age, and other factors such as each person's unique brain and body biochemical reactions to stress, pain, fear, and injury play a role in people's trained responses. Making sense of the chaos that crime brings to their lives moves victims along the path of reconstruction (Jenkins, 1999). Often the ability to hope and love is based on the belief that there is some meaning and control in life.

Many common trauma symptoms of crime victims are identifiable. Victim Advocates need to be prepared to assist victims with multiple needs, as well as the needs of their support persons. In addition to common crisis reactions, some victims may experience some or all of the symptoms of Post Traumatic Stress Disorder (PTSD): rage, panic, depression, nightmares, dissociation, flashbacks, withdrawal, loss of control, substance abuse, memory distortion, sleep and eating disorders, and extreme anxiety (Ochberg, 2003; Walker, 2006). Knowing these are possible long-term reactions provides a map in preparing for both the initial and intermediate outcomes victims may seek to address (Kass-Bartelmes & Rutherford; 2004). [See Exhibit 7a for a sample activities manual/traumatic emotions cheat sheet] There are many theories of victim trauma and recovery. The key is to identify the progression upon which to build outcomes in an initial, intermediate, and long-term sequence in order to enable and encourage the victim's own resiliency.

There are many theories of victim trauma and recovery. The key is to identify the progression upon which to build outcomes in an initial, intermediate, and long-term sequence in order to enable and encourage the victim's own resiliency.

Victim Advocates can, at a minimum, listen, debrief, and clarify the victims' feelings and situations, identify coping strategies and options, outline common coping actions (e.g. avoid anxiety triggering situations, keep busy, ask for help), and assist the victims in returning to their previous levels of functioning. There are many models of response to trauma. Most include a few key building blocks in helping victims live without being controlled by the victimization experience, including promoting hope, empowerment, and the victim's understanding that he or she was not at fault (U.S. Department of Health and Human Services, 2005). [For sample activities and outputs for healing outcomes, see Exhibit 4b]

What are the primary outcomes for Justice?

The majority of victims must seek a sense of justice and acceptance without the benefit of a tidy justice system conclusion.

Justice is an elusive concept because no two victims are the same, or define justice similarly. Against this backdrop, victims initially seek understanding of their roles and options in the justice process. The motto: "Victim Rights: Every Victim, Every Time," is valuable when victim participation and information are desired in a prosecuted case. In reality, however, the majority of victims must seek a sense of justice and acceptance without the benefit of a tidy justice system conclusion.

For many victims, justice is primarily about legal assistance with divorce, child custody, protection orders, or related financial issues (Victim Rights Law Center, 2008). For other victims, justice is about the choices, services, and systems that provide acknowledgment of and recovery from

Outcome Model for Justice

the wrong done to them. Offender accountability and punishment, when possible, are usually added forces for victim recovery. Victims attaining the second tier of intermediate outcomes often end a phase of their victimization experience, allowing them to look forward in life with hope.

Fairness, dignity, and respect are critical aspects of justice for victims. Every jurisdiction pursues justice differently. Many officials seem to be operating their own "M.A.S.H." unit of justice as they attempt to keep up with the avalanche of cases and constraints.

Victim Advocates should have the skill, knowledge, and experience to guide victims through the justice labyrinth. Adequate training and familiarity with the process and system officials is critical to providing the necessary information upon which victims will make informed decisions. This must be done within the constraints of the law, and unless licensed to do so, without practicing law by giving individual advice.

The more written information that is specific to the victim, the better. It is helpful to have prepared a variety of topics defined and explained topics in standardized format that can be provided as needed. For example, a comprehensive trial preparation booklet is unnecessary and burdensome for a victim only needing to know what to expect during initial investigator and prosecutor interviews. A slow and clear explanation, with highlighting of key points in writing is often helpful. However, asking each victim what they want to know and how they want it presented is ideal. Written information is advisable instead of presuming that verbal explanations will be recalled and

Written information is advisable instead of presuming that verbal explanations will be recalled and understood days later.

understood days later. Partnerships and protocols with other victim service providers, attorneys, and justice officials, who can provide more information to victims specific to the interviews, hearings, or other proceedings are valuable and should be developed and maintained. [See Exhibit 4c for a Justice Outcome Model with sample activities and outputs for each outcome]

What are the primary outcomes for Restitution (Financial Recovery)?

Financial recovery is also a core victim need. This means meeting basic human needs for health care, child care, housing, food, and clothing. It starts with meeting emergency and initial needs, such as costs for counseling and treatment of injuries, medicine, repairing damage to homes and cars, transportation and gasoline, food, etc., with utilities and moving needs often following. For some victims, lost or damaged clothing and tools required for work are the critical needs. Depending on the qualifications and restrictions for applying for the state victim compensation program, immediate information and assistance may be required to protect the victim's right to access state reimbursement. Depending on the state, for example, a police report may need to be filed within 72 hours of the crime.

Victims might be paid early by insurance or receive restitution from offenders during early court hearings. Usually, however, recovery may take years or never happen. The priority in meeting ongoing financial needs may include assistance so victims can return to work to school to maintain

Outcome Model for Restitution

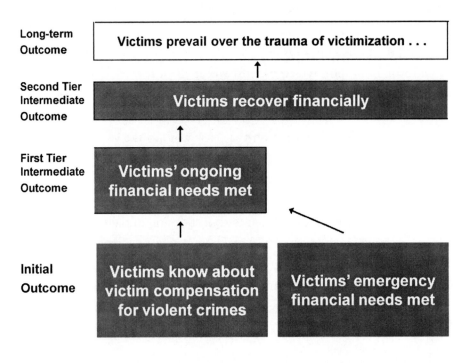

scholarships and loans. Common sense and the teachings in nearly all cultures and religions of the world require an offender to compensate the victim for harm caused. Regardless of the severity of the victims' trauma and harm, or the financial need of the victims, the definition of fairness and obligation of the offenders to make things right require that the perpetrators' financial obligations last until the losses are paid in full. Other sources of victim financial recovery may include civic clubs (e.g. Lions Club helping with new eyeglasses), civil law suits, victim service program emergency funds, public assistance, church benevolent funds, and court-ordered attachments of offender assets and bonds.

The concept of victim recovery as an outcome can include more than just money. For many victims the dollars are critical, and for others they are merely symbolic. For some victims, hearing their victimization acknowledged and remorse expressed by the offenders is as important as any monetary repayment. Similarly, offenders doing court-supervised community service, victim-determined charity work, or work directly for the victim (e.g. yard work), may be the chosen restitution outcome that serves to restore their sense of relationship, trust, and neighborhood. [For a restitution outcome model with sample activities and outputs, see Exhibit 4d]

Do different kinds of victims have different outcomes?

Recovery from grief is unique to each individual, yet commonalities exist. Broad outlines of grief therapy exist, while counselors adopt individualized interventions. Likewise, broad victim outcomes exist although no two victims have identical needs (Michigan Crime Victim Services Commission, 2003). Victimology informs us that natural disaster survivors, military combat survivors, and crime victims experience some common trauma symptoms. Even so, crime victims have more in common with each other, and sexual assault survivors have more in common with others who have been sexually assaulted. Even sexual assault programs differ by purpose, resources, structure, and jurisdiction, depending on the needs of the local population (Witwer, Emmerling, & McManus, 2003). For example, as different as sexual assault programs are, and as different as outcome logic models will look for each unique program (Texas Association Against Sexual Assault, 2003), some common outcomes likely exist for victims not to feel alone, to feel believed, and to identify whether they were sexually assaulted.

Add to the variety of outcomes and services the influencing factors of language, culture, rural or urban, or living on a military base, and the complexities in determining and meeting outcomes grow even for similar victimizations. Yet, as varied as these programs are, the programs have

The definition of fairness and obligation of the offenders to make things right require that the perpetrators' financial obligations last until the losses are paid in full.

Consider the variety and commonalities of victims served by the following:

1. Hospital-based sexual assault programs for adult victims

2. Programs for sexually abused children and their non-offending parents

3. Sexual Assault Response Team (SART) focus on single interview process

4. Rape Crisis Centers focusing on operating a one-stop service location

5. Sexual assault counseling programs

6. Rape crisis hotlines providing short-term counseling and information contacts

7. Sexual assault prevention services for college campuses

8. Counseling and assistance programs for adults molested as children

9. Peer support groups for survivors

10. Clinical support groups for survivors of sexual trafficking

a sisterhood which reveals some common issues, safety concerns, recovery patterns, response themes, and therapeutic strategies (Sullivan, Coats, 2000). The needs of sexual assault survivors are diverse, yet there seem to be some common outcomes in this web of individual and inter-related needs (RAINN, 2008). For example, sexual assault survivors often desire to reduce trauma symptoms and trauma triggers, and commonly share a desire to recover and heal their emotional and physical selves.

The more common the crime, the more likely victims are able to have similar outcomes. The more common the outcomes, the more likely that particular activities and processes, (e.g. therapeutic support group) will benefit more participants (Newmark, 2006). However, as hard as we work to do the most good for the most victims, we must be equally cautious not to group victims with overly prescriptive interventions. Even with a 95% anticipated or historical rate of certain activities benefiting victim participants, not all victims will have their needs met and Victim Advocates still have to make choices regarding how to produce the greatest value with the resources available (Pennsylvania Commission on Crime and Delinquency, 2003).

The general goal of victim advocacy is to help victims progress to the highest levels of the longer-term outcomes they desire. Some advocates distinguish between person-directed outcomes that are clinical (e.g. reducing symptoms of trauma), functional outcomes (e.g. physical healing and improvement in daily living skills), and personal priorities and dreams of the victim (e.g. moving closer to family or wanting to live alone) (National Center on Outcome Resources, 2001). The recovery process is uneven. People's lives are not perfectly ordered and neither is recovery dependably linear. Each step in the model is a piece of the puzzle. For example, helping victims document restitution, receive court orders for it, and collect it, are likely part of their recovery processes to prevail over the trauma caused by a property violation.

Domestic violence victims often say, "I just want it [the violence] to stop." Experience informs us that domestic violence survivors not only describe similar needs, but they often answer with similar words and concepts to the question, "What does healing look like for you?"

Domestic violence victims often say, "I just want it [the violence] to stop." Experience informs us that domestic violence survivors not only describe similar needs, but they often answer with similar words and concepts to the question, "What does healing look like for you?" Some common domestic violence survivor outcomes include: safety, improved relationships and intimacy with others, reduced traumatic emotions and behaviors, increased sense of empowerment, self-control, self-esteem, and a desire to be free of violence and to be able to trust others again (Zollinger, Wolfe, Ray, Walker, Paige, & Gross, 2007).

Other victims have commonalities as well. Homicide survivors often talk about trying to learn to love again or live again with an unfilled hole in their lives. So, prevailing over their victimization has a different meaning for different kinds of victims. Each special victim population shares the big picture goals that are hard to measure and attribute, but toward which Victim Advocates can help victims strive. Following are some ideas of specific victim populations and programs' special understanding of what it means to prevail over the trauma of their victimization:

1. by living a life free from violence (Domestic Violence)
2. by achieving personal healing (Sexual Assault)
3. with safety, healing, justice, and financial recovery (Violent & Property)
4. by living a new life with love and loss (Homicide)
5. through the healing of our spiritual being (Victim Ministry Program) [See Exhibit 4e]
6. by finding a positive experience from the crime (Victim Impact Panel Program) [See Exhibit 4f]
7. by making more informed decisions (Domestic Violence Support Group) [See Exhibit 4g]
8. by freeing burdensome emotions (Victim Offender Dialogue Program) [See Exhibits 4h and 4i]

What are the primary influencing factors for outcomes?

Many influencing factors affect the efforts of victims and Victim Advocates. Domestic violence victims have significant common influencing factors compared to bank robbery victims who don't have prior relationships or history with the offenders. In addition, each initial and intermediate outcome has influencing factors. Whether a victim continues to feel alone after a crime may depend on the victim's ability to share the experience. Furthermore, the sensitivity, voice tone, and compassion of responding family, friends, faith leaders, social community, and the Victim Advocate, may also play a role in the victim's healing.

The five overarching outcomes have a myriad of issues that influence progress, including those that are:

1. Victim related—Economic resources; articulateness; knowledge and prejudices about the justice system; family and social support; language and cultural barriers; geographic and distance issues; current and previous trauma experiences
2. Crime related—Frequency and severity of theft or violence; relationship to offender; arrest and conviction; degree and type of injury; type of victimization
3. System related—Treatment by justice officials or media (Michigan Coalition, 2007 & 2004); bond level; arrest laws and implementa-

Factors That Influence Outcomes

Victim—resources, opinions, resiliency, support, language, knowledge, abilities

Case—frequency, severity, relationship to event, type of crime/problem

System—treatment by officials, media, protocols, funding, laws

Program—access (barriers, structure (caseload), process (timeliness)

Environmental—weather, geography, politics, culture, community values

tion; response protocols (e.g. Does Child Protection Services investigate all domestic violence reports when children are present?)

4. Program related—Access to program; structure differences such as the Victim Advocate intervention skills, comprehension and utilization of outcomes, and their caseload burden that limits the time and talent available to help the victim; the process of timely and user-friendly interactions with victims.

5. Environment related—Community support; geographic barriers; weather variables; economic influences; political climate.

What do you need to know when you are identifying outcomes?

The choice of outcomes is important. Outcomes are the primary goals of all programs, services, and financial expenditures. They will determine which program activities are useful and which services the agency should no longer prioritize. Select them with care, using the guidance of victims and stakeholders. Do not be afraid to learn from trial and error. Even after victim outcomes have been chosen, they need to be monitored and reviewed with vigilance. Programs should select the fewest core outcomes possible while remaining true to the victims served, in order to reduce complexity of the model and evaluation process.

Initial outcomes are the most likely to be influenced and made attainable by victim services, so programs should focus on them. These might include crisis intervention, emotional stabilization, support from family and friends, knowledge about the justice system and involvement options, medical treatment, emergency financial bills, protective shelter, and helping victims feel believed by responding officers and hospital staff. The most important outcomes to address are the ones most important to victims.

The three parts in creating an outcome, your change statement are:

1. The change or desired effect (e.g. increase, decrease, maintain, improve, reduce, expand, create)
2. In what (e.g. attitude, behavior, condition, knowledge, insight, skill, status in an area of safety, healing, justice, or financial recovery)
3. For whom/what (e.g. individual, family, community members)

For example, a good goal might be to increase safety behaviors for youth ages 9-12 while in emergency shelter for when they leave (Francis, 2000).

What criteria should I use when selecting outcomes?

Some considerations in selecting outcomes include whether they:

1. are endorsed and owned by victims and stakeholders (most important criteria)

Choosing Victim Outcomes

- Predict what victims need to believe, know, have, do, or become as a result of the outcome
- Use key words to show change: new, increased, improved, decreased, create, etc.
- Estimate the degree to which the victim or situation can realistically be influenced
- Use initial outcomes and know the whole model
- Understand that similar victims can have dissimilar outcomes

Some sample questions to ask:

1. What difference do we think our services make for victims?
2. Why do we do what we do?
3. What do we want to be true for victims after they receive our services?
4. If we do these activities, then what will victims believe, know, have, do or become as a result?
5. What change outside of our program do we want our activities to create?

2. help in disclosing program weakness and strength (influence effectiveness)

3. communicate the value and the story of changing victims' lives (e.g. can they be explained to non-professionals?)

4. are influenced directly (are actionable) within a reasonable time frame by program activities and services

5. help attain more complex and later outcomes

6. have indicators that are measurable

7. are well-defined in scope

8. represent common victim needs (i.e. affect more than a few victims)

9. are significant in affecting the desired change in victims

10. reflect the program's values and priorities

Humorous application of an outcome logic model

Below is a humorous (do not look for perfect accuracy) use of the outcome model that David S. Adams, PhD., applied to the song "Santa Claus is Coming to Town." The long-term outcomes of good mental health and high self-esteem are attained through intermediate outcomes (improved goodness and niceness) (Adams, D., 2009).

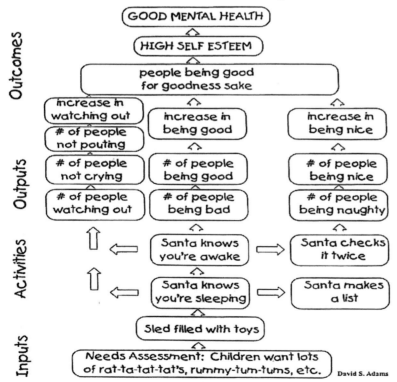

Chapter 4 Summary: A Victim Outcome Logic Model

Victims have four overarching need areas: safety, healing, justice, and financial restitution. Using the input, activity, output, and outcome design of the logic model, the general progression of victim need is illustrated for all four areas. Victims of similar types of crimes often have common outcome goals. The victim outcome logic model is a guide for Victim Advocates to understand which services, and in what sequence, might help victims reach their individual needs. Since the advocacy process does not happen in a vacuum, it is important to understand how interactions are influenced by factors from within each victim, the systems involved, and within the program design and operation. To begin a logic model, you start by selecting the outcomes which victims need, which you can reasonably influence, and which you have the resources and activities to attain.

Chapter 5
Measuring Outcome Success
You cannot measure what you cannot count

What is an outcome indicator?

Outcome indicators are milestones on your journey to the outcome. Outcome measures, on the other hand, are specific destinations. Indicators are the objectives that inform you of your performance levels and proximity to reaching the outcomes. For example, a flight leaving from Los Angeles bound for Korea is not likely to stop in New York along the way. Landing in New York is an indicator that a successful flight to East Asia is unlikely that day, but a stop in Honolulu indicates progress toward the destination. Smaller measures along the way to determine performance could be air speed, direction, fuel consumption, and absence of trouble lights in the cockpit. Good data is just as important in victim advocacy since there are many variables affecting the information you are collecting on the way. Taking measurements and asking data questions means you are doing some level of research (Messing, T.J., 2007-2008).

Once you have selected outcomes, the next step is determining a process to know whether you have succeeded in reaching them or are even heading in the right direction. Having valid and routine indicators of success is critical. For example, if a victim requests assistance in reducing sleep disturbances, some indicators of success may include increasing length of sleep without waking, reduced nightmares, or increasing ability to sleep without lights on.

The value and role of good outcome indicators is informing you where you are on the journey map—the degree to which you are making progress toward your destination, and establishing when you have arrived at your outcome. However, accurate measures of irrelevant indicators are not helpful, so another goal is to determine the validity of your indicators before you begin measuring them (Coldren, Bynum, & Thome, 1991).

The essential questions are:

1. What are you trying to find out?
2. How do you collect the information?
3. How will you know if you have arrived at an outcome?

- What gets measured gets done.

- If you don't measure results, you can't tell success from failure.

- If you can't see success, you can't reward it.

- If you can't reward success, you're probably rewarding failure.

- If you can't see success, you can't learn from it.

- If you can't recognize failure, you can't correct it.

- If you can demonstrate results, you can win public support.

Osborne and Gaebler, 1992

4. How do you distinguish between two victims, as to who arrived at the outcome?

An indicator should provide information as to whether or not you have been successful, and if not, to what degree you need to improve (Michigan Public Health Institute, 1998). The most important criteria for an indicator are its clear and precise relationship to the outcome and its accuracy as a measure. For example, an ambiguous indicator for a safety outcome in a domestic violence shelter kids program is: "children will know safety responses." Is there enough clarity in the indicator for two different evaluators to agree whether or not the children met the safety outcome? It is unlikely. A better option for this indicator is: "Every child between the age of 5 and 11 in the shelter for at least three days can roleplay calling 911 and roleplay running out of the room (or out of the house if safety allows) when one person is threatening or physically abusing the other."

Some examples of indicators for the emotional healing outcome of violent crime victims are changes in frequency and severity of sleep problems, nightmares, and flashbacks; participating in social events; accomplishing household tasks; and enjoying hobbies. Spiritual healing outcome indicators may include frequency and depth of victim's ability to experience oneness with God, inner spiritual peace, recovery from grief, and an ability to provide comfort to others in need. Other faith-specific indicators may also be appropriate, such as prayer and scripture reading levels and participation in sacraments, faith-tradition events, or group worship.

Spiritual healing outcome indicators may include frequency and depth of victim's ability to experience oneness with God, inner spiritual peace, recovery from grief, and an ability to provide comfort to others in need.

What are some criteria for selecting an indicator?

There are a number of considerations in choosing an appropriate indicator (McNamara, 1997-2006):

1. Valuable—Is it an important measurement for the mission?
2. Cost-effective—Is it within the resources of the program to collect?
3. Specific—Is it directly tied to only one outcome?
4. Representative—Does it reflect victims seeking that outcome?
5. Acceptable—Is it non-offensive and meaningful to ask?
6. Significant—Is it statistically significant?
7. Unambiguous—Is the result interpreted similarly by different evaluators?
8. Sensitive—Can it detect small variations?
9. Timely—Is it too early or late for measuring the progress?
10. Unbiased—What other human factors influence the outcome?

Additionally, the usefulness of an indicator in demonstrating impact is a consideration.

1. *Reactions and feelings* are early indicators that victim outcomes are

being met, but the least reliable measurements that your service will have a lasting impact on their lives.

2. *Learning* that reflects enhanced attitudes, perceptions, and new knowledge is a useful level of outcome evaluation information.

3. *Changes in skills* that demonstrate the victim applied the learning and insights to enhance their behaviors are a better indicator of lasting service value.

4. *Effectiveness* of improved performance resulting from the enhanced behaviors is the best indicator, and the most difficult to document reliably.

Indicators must be appropriate and impact the desired outcome. Having indicator data is crucial because, as the old saying goes, "without data you're just another person with an opinion." This is true whether you are measuring improvements in victims' lives by speed, degree, or individual value. Indicators measure degrees of goal attainment and can often be reported as numbers, percentages, amounts (volume), or ratings. Using plots and graphs to show indicator data over time can help connect the dots in a more visual manner.

Common Forms of Indicators		
Form of Indicator	**How to Compute**	**Examples**
Number	Count each one fitting the criteria	Number of victims who received protection orders
Percentage	Divide by the total number (above) by total of all fitting the criteria	Percent of victims reporting fewer nightmares/flashbacks
Amount	Measure the volume of something	Amount of victim compensation/restitution received
Rating	Assign an informed, subjective score	Rating of a rape victim's increase in self-confidence according to tone of voice

What are common outcome data sources?

Outcome data sources are where the information (your indicator data) about your victims resides. The value and veracity of the indicators depend largely on where the information comes from and how it is collected (Morley, Vinson, & Hatry, 2001). Usually, selecting the right source of information depends on its availability, the time and labor costs to collect it, and its accuracy. Once you have decided which outcome data source to use, it is important to document the reasons for the choices made and any known reliability variables. Listed below are some options and issues for where to look for victim information to determine levels of succes in

Outcome data sources are where the information (your indicator data) about your victims resides.

Outcome Data Sources

- Case records
- Victims
- Observable conditions
- Data files
- Family
- Documents
- Public
- Colleagues

independent indicators.

1. Existing information in the program or another agency

Victim case records and data files (paper or electronic) are often good sources because they lay out the victims' information and how it was collected. Important initial outcome data (e.g. whether a victim emergency need was met or not) is also often available in case records.

Documents may also be available from prosecutors, courts, counselors, etc. for other perspectives and for victim information after program services have ended. However, the available data might not be carefully recorded, appropriate, for the correct time period, or available due to confidentiality or due to labor costs to get the data.

2. Individual victims, families, and peers

Victims and family members are often ideal sources of information, though their knowledge may be insufficient or biased. Victims may also be reluctant to share personal details or changes in their lives with their families. It may be advisable to separate the outcome questions from the quality and satisfaction questions to clarify outcome success levels. For example, victims can be asked outcome questions prior to the sentencing hearing, and then asked the access, structure, process, and satisfaction questions at case closing. We measure to improve lives, not take credit or blame.

Others who know the victims, such as counselors, support group members, or their co-workers, may also provide information when suitable and appropriate confidentiality releases are in place. One of the advantages is that when others provide information, the victims do not feel pressured to give the right answers. However, the concerns about biased and inaccurate responses remain.

3. Physical and environmental conditions

Some indicators are detectable through observers' senses, such as seeing identifiable changes in relationships or in the victims' confidence. However, observable data may not be as clear as it seems, due to masking of true beliefs or feelings, and it can be interpreted differently even by trained observers.

What are common outcome data collection methods?

The data collection method is the decision as to how to extract the information from the source.

The data collection method is the decision as to how to extract the information from the source (Sullivan & Alexy, 2001). Some options:

1. Records, documents, and data files review

Collecting information already recorded in the agency's files is often convenient since there are no access or consent problems, and any bias in the collection is more obvious because you know why and how it collected. The primary issue is often whether the right information is available. If the information is in another agency's files, it may be unavailable, for the wrong period, etc.

2. <u>Written questionnaires, surveys, and checklists</u>

Some advantages to surveys are that they can be specific to the outcome measures and often offered to victims anonymously and conveniently (Newmark, 2001). Unless routinely completed in person (e.g. in the shelter, office, or courthouse), the return rate and reliability decrease dramatically. Mailed surveys also assume a level of literacy and language proficiency that may not be accurate, and presume a level of safety that may be problematic. Safety issues include endangering victims or compromising confidentiality, particularly when the correspondence goes to a residence where the offenders live, could visit, or have access to the mail. Mailed written surveys normally have a low return rate and thus cannot be statistically used as representative samples of respondents, since possibly only the happiest and angriest return them. However, with precautions for safety as a priority, and recognition that literacy, language, and confidentiality are also issues to deal with, mailed surveys are often the easiest to implement [See Exhibits 5, 5a, and 5b for sample surveys].

Some key issues to consider with surveys and other collection methods are informed consent, confidentiality, and anonymity. When seeking quality and outcome information from victims, the more personally invasive the information and process, and the more significant the use of the results for evaluating personnel and program, the more important it is for victims to understand the process. This is an ethical continuum.

Consent is critical. Victims should always know they have the option to participate, ask questions, and withdraw at anytime. When their data will be used to make significant decisions, victims should have more information about the purposes, uses, processes, risks, and benefits of participating in the information collection. For example, if staff members' personnel evaluation scores or merit raises are impacted by the victims' feedback, then the victims should be informed that their responses would have that use.

If you state their responses are confidential, you may know who is responding but you are committing to keeping their identity secret. You cannot reveal any information that could link their responses to them personally. For example, you cannot use identifying information such as names, addresses, and response information that could distinguish them. In many communities, a victim survey response noted as being from a family member in a murder case from a particular month is identifying the family involved, if not the exact person responding.

Committing to anonymous victim responses means you must have a

---

Survey Return Ideas

- Color Code survey by staff or program
- Complete surveys promptly (within days, not weeks)
- Add signed notes in colored ink asking for specific victims' feedback
- Buy free return postage on mailed survey envelopes
- Expect 4-5% return rate of non-representative replies
- Include surveys in final case information mailings
- Advise victims to expect surveys
- Use folding mailers
- Insert free gifts (magnets, calendars, palm cards)

Victim Survey Options

- Surveys can be done by:
- Mail with self-addressed, stamped return envelope
- Website of program being surveyed (must offer hard copy option)
- Personal interviews by staff at shelter, court, office, etc.
- In-person in writing at shelter, court, office, etc. (with sealed return box)
- Through e-mails (never in cases where the abusers have access to the victims' e-mail)
- Personal interviews by telephone with volunteers or staff
- Personal interviews at the end of calls to crisis lines

process to ensure that you will not know who responds to your surveys or other collection methods. This is both a practical issue of gathering information without victims identifying themselves to you in the process, and a problem of perception. For example, victims may wonder if the lock box for their survey is opened immediately after they depart, or suspect the numbers on their surveys (that you use to link staff or programs) are unique identifiers of them.

Some issues with surveys:

1. Some victims of violence (e.g. robbery) may instead self-identify as property crime victims, so it is helpful to have staff write the types of crime on the surveys before they are mailed. Alternately, add examples or definitions of the crime categories used so the victims understand which types of crime to mark.

2. Victims may report not receiving services that were actually provided. For example, victims may report that they received no emergency money, yet the program has signed receipts. One solution is to verify that all staff refer to the money for victims using the exact words on the survey, such as "emergency money." Using the same key words or references during services will reduce the confusion in victim survey responses.

3. Face-to-face interviews

Although not anonymous, face-to-face interviews have some advantages: friendly locations to meet can be selected; questions can be explained or responses clarified; nonverbal behaviors that indicate a need for clarity can be observed; and victims are less likely to skip any questions. Additional victim services are also possible when victims express unresolved concerns or new problems.

However, there is a possible inflating of positive responses or minimizing negatives since people are generally uncomfortable giving poor evaluations when their identity is not anonymous. Again, program improvement is the goal of the inverviews, not giving credit or laying blame. Also, face-to-face interviews take more staff or volunteer time and more organizational time to schedule, which makes them more expensive. Some negative victim variables may include being less articulate, or being speech/language impaired.

4. Telephone interviews

Telephone interviews may help victims feel more anonymous and more comfortable responding candidly from their own home. Interviewers can encourage feedback, resulting in less data missing, particularly if the interviewer is not the Victim Advocate assigned the case. Personal contacts can identify unresolved concerns and result in additional services.

Calls are cheaper than face-to-face interviews but more expensive than

Program improvement is the goal of the inverviews, not giving credit or laying blame.

mailed surveys. They also run the risk of family members listening and inhibiting victim responses. Pre-arranging call times with victims increases the likelihood of completing the interview, but is more time consuming and expensive. Also, victims without telephones or call screening are excluded.

5. Other collection methods

Observation of victims to evaluate success of reaching outcomes may be possible for shelters, rape crisis centers, and other in-person service providers. The environment may influence interactions, responses, and behaviors. Although hard to aggregate, examples of using observation to document victims feeling less alone due to the support of the Victim Advocate include when the victims:

a. Express gratitude and say thank you

b. Demonstrate gratitude by initiating a hug or handshake

c. Ask for the same Advocate each time

d. Ask for additional information (i.e. exhibit trust)

e. Ask the Advocate to remain with them through the process

Case studies can depict victims' experiences of input, activity, process, and results, at least through the closing of the case. They can be effective storytelling tools to outsiders, with appropriate releases and confidentiality protections, but are time consuming to collect, organize, and describe.

Focus groups of six to eight victims can establish common impressions quickly and reliably, and are efficient ways to get a wider range and depth of information in a short time. However, they cannot provide individual victim outcome attainment measures and are limited by the group dynamics and skills of the facilitators.

Data is only as good as it is accurate, meaningful, and available. It is helpful to create quantitative (output) and qualitative (outcome) data management systems, and correlate the two. As programs vary greatly, the ideal system will provide tailor-made options for outcomes linked to the types and levels of activities and their outputs. In other words, reduced or unrelated actions (e.g. educational presentations to elementary school children) lead to less valuable or lower levels of outputs (e.g. fewer Victim Compensation applications provided) which likely affect the level of financial recovery outcomes attained for adult victims of sexual assault. Determining the correlation between specific activities with outcome indicators is extremely useful in explaining and tracking changes in outcomes, however, the links may only be recognizable over months or years. The difficulty of the task is that much information is needed, and it takes time, ability, and interest to analyze the data.

The inferred connection from work done to realizing victim benefits is

Considerations in collecting outcome results include:

1. Confidentiality—Adhering to victim release and contact parameters

2. Anonymity—Not identifying or linking responses to particular victims

3. Safety—Assuring that victims' participation will not cause them harm

4. Usefulness—Asking only needed information

5. Respect—Asking only appropriate questions (outcomes are personal)

6. Diversity—Insuring that a mix of persons receive, understand, and respond (e.g. age, citizenship status, gender, disabilities, literacy, income)

7. Helpfulness—Providing a process that does not confuse victims about their situations, services, progress, and value (e.g. reverse questions may confuse victims or make them feel tricked, so they may be unwilling to complete the form)

> *However, some effort is better than no effort in tracking outcome journeys. The real telltale signs of commitment to improving outcomes are effective monitoring and evaluation.*

an excellent management and motivating tool. It takes inquisitiveness and time to analyze and estimate the links between activities and outcomes. Even experts can miss key data due to sampling problems and the plethora of influencing factors.

However, some effort is better than no effort in tracking outcome journeys. The real telltale signs of commitment to improving outcomes are effective monitoring and evaluation. Simply reporting data, even accurate data, does not demonstrate the value of using outcomes to manage the quality and results of programs. Of course, the number of victim and program differences, influencing factors, and the time necessary to collect, process, report, and analyze data can be discouraging. The challenge is to be a leader in improving outcomes that make differences in victims' lives through comprehensive organizational designs that include *ongoing* analysis and adaptations.

What can outcomes not do?

As valuable as outcomes are in telling the stories of changed lives and improving the quality of services with good indicator forms, sources, and methods, outcomes do have their limitations. There are critical and foundational issues that outcomes cannot improve.

"The methodology of outcome measurement is descriptive, not experimental, and thus has inherent limitations. Careful selection of outcome indicators and quality information from reliable sources will still not 'prove' some things. Outcome data will NOT:

1. Show whether this is the right outcome to measure;
2. Prove statistically that the program caused the outcome;
3. Explain why this level of outcome was achieved;
4. By themselves, tell what to change to improve the outcome;
5. Determine whether funders should invest in the outcomes" (United Way, 1998)

What issues exist in reporting outcomes?

When reporting outcome results, the context is significant. Variables that may need to be considered and noted:

1. Examples of services and activities that are linked to the outcomes
2. Time between the crimes and when the information is collected
3. Time between when victim advocacy started and when data is collected
4. Information sources and limitations
5. Collection methods (e.g. phone, in-person, mail, and guideline for excluding any victim from the evaluation process)

6. Number of respondents

7. Number of cases, primary victims, and total victims assisted during the period

8. Comparison of response percentage with victims and/or cases served

9. Dates of reporting periods (e.g. monthly, quarterly, or annually)

10. Significant influencing factors (e.g. changes in services, partners, staff, activities) and important limitations (e.g. indicator or survey item changes)

11. Degree to which the programs are able to influence each indicator used

12. Notations if and when data cannot explain the results

The response rate and volume are also important. Some evaluators' general statistical rule for survey accuracy is that higher than a 75% response rate is acceptable, between 50-75% is questionable, and below 50% is useless (Hendricks, M., 2007). This is because certain people are prone to answer or never answer surveys, just as certain people tend to answer only positively or negatively. With voluntary and self-selecting respondents the problem is knowing whether or not the people who responded accurately represent all victims assisted. Alternatives include a random sampling (e.g. every 25th victim) with extra effort to get the full sampling to respond. In early stages of data collection, the integrity of the process of collecting is more important than causality. Once a dependable process is in place, the reliability of the data can be prioritized.

How can you make outcome reports more useful?

An outcome report is only as good as it is accurate, useful, understandable, and interesting. To help the audience evaluate outcome results, reporting may include comparisons:

1. To the severity of the problems/conditions without the program

2. To national or state standards

3. To similar victims receiving comparable services elsewhere

4. To victim functioning levels based on pre- and post-service tests (e.g. safety, healing, justice, and financial stress between entering and leaving the program)

To help data be more useful, report both the percent of potential respondents as well as the percent reporting improvement (of those who responded). For example, getting restitution paid is only an outcome success when a victim actually had a financial loss. So, if 100 victims are assisted, of which 34% experienced a financial loss and of those 50% recovered restitution from the offender, then the outcome report could note that "of victims who had a financial loss, 50% percent had their needs met," rather

Reporting Outcomes
- Indictors are fluid
- Survey responses should reflect all assisted
- Data should include reliability factors
- Goal is at least 80% positive responses

than reporting "only 17% of victims (of the total of 100) had their financial needs reimbursed."

Reports should include some assessment of the data. Inform the audience why results may be as they are, and what the program does to refine, improve, create, or discard the process (activities, collection method, etc.). It is not always helpful to use words like "error" or "poor" results. Rather, point out areas found to be "challenging" and "opportunities for improvement."

Outcome reports should state inconsistencies and reliability factors of results. Outcome data comparisons can list pertinent factors and disclaimers of variables inherent with the report or data comparisons, such as definitions of service, types of victimization, types of victims (e.g. child, adult, language barriers, disabled, etc.), geographical distances from justice services, etc. Small sample numbers or returned surveys/interviews are important reliability factors. Even if a sampling is small, year-to-year comparisons of responses may supply evidence of consistency.

Reporting the number of quality and outcome surveys returned compared to the total number of victims assisted may not be a fair sampling. Many victims have only peripheral contact with programs. For example, victims may request victim compensation applications, parking or hearing information, or only attend hearings with family members or friends. A more accurate representation of the benefits of services may be the total number of cases or the number of primary victims who received surveys or had other opportunities to evaluate services. A minimum threshold to include victims in the survey process and data analysis could be at least a half an hour contact by staff with a victim in person or by telephone (except hotline services), or at least two correspondence contacts, hearing notices, or housing assistance meetings.

Adding questions regarding the treatment or responsiveness of law enforcement, prosecutors, and other allied fields is a reasonable approach, but will make an evaluation longer. Also, victims may confuse personnel and law enforcement, prosecutors, and victim services. In addition, the options for responses in interviews or on surveys may mean different things to different victims, and control groups are not usually available since services cannot be refused to some victims for comparison purposes.

Pre- and post-testing of knowledge or emotional strength are valuable measurement tools. In some situations this is not possible since it is not appropriate or ethical to ask a victim in crisis to answer baseline questions for future comparison purposes. An initial treatment plan may be a better tool since the presenting problems can be compared later to see if the needs were met.

Numerous victims and cases may need to be excluded from particular reporting ratios, follow-up contacts, and service evaluations. Some examples of potential circumstances to stop or alternate contacts:

1. Contact information is known to be wrong or unavailable

2. Further victim service contacts would be unsafe

3. Minimal contacts and interactions occur between program staff and the victim

4. There are multiple family members or business employees with whom contact is purely redundant (recognizing that even close family members may require distinct services, react differently to the same service, and need their own opportunity to evaluate the quality and benefit of services)

5. A victim requests no further contact

6. Businesses or organizations have so many victimizations that specific cases are not individually monitored

7. Other special circumstances approved and documented by a supervisor

Measuring victim outcomes to evaluate program performance raises other problems as well. Some researchers will not measure trauma symptoms as outcomes because they are too fluid. Symptoms often increase or appear a year after preliminary reductions appear on time-specific outcome measures. For example, the trigger for a victim's fear or symptoms of Post-Traumatic Stress Disorder (PTSD) can occur anytime, such as while watching the evening news. Measuring an individual victim's outcome is a single snapshot in time and may not reflect a general increase or reduction. However, trends in favorable rating for all respondents can show progress.

What is your North Star through all this?

Do not be discouraged if 80% of your results derive from 20% of your effort. The value of outcomes depends on strong leadership and a commitment to quality victim advocacy. Even a simple outcome logic model is enough to focus program direction and related activities toward achieving outcome goals. Remember, the point is not research; it is improving victims' lives through improved access, structure, process, and outcomes. As noted earlier, your greatest benefit may come from your ongoing efforts (with victims, collaboration, etc.) to define and refine your victim outcome and program goals, and the time and effort to try to improve and measure your progress. Victims' and Victim Advocates' bad days are not so hopeless when we feel confident we are heading in the right direction.

The primary reasons to embrace outcomes are to enhance service effectiveness in improving victim's lives and to increase decision accountability. The board of directors, volunteers, and staff should know that their decisions are based on the effectiveness and efficiency in reaching victim outcomes.

Good outcome management means having a culture and a process which results in positive and improving outcomes. After finding the needs of victims toward which activities are directed, the primary tasks are to serve those needs and to accurately measure achievement in order that the measures can be utilized and implemented to improve results. Your slogan can be, "Our culture prioritizes victim outcomes and the processes to improve them."

Ultimately, all the designing, monitoring, measuring, interpretation of data, and adapting of services rests on the attitude, ability, and passion of volunteers and staff delivering the victim advocacy. The same applies to programs and evaluations. True accountability is internal.

Chapter 5 Summary: Measuring Outcome Success

To know if you are reaching your victim outcomes, you need indicators of

Accountability

True Victim Advocate accountability is internal—a passion for caring and action that results in measureable victim outcomes

True program accountability is internal—accessibility, necessary services, respect for unique victims, and demonstrable change in victims' lives progress that you can measure. Some questions to consider when determining these signposts include: the value of the indicator (e.g. is the indicator directly linked to the outcome?); the level of change considered success (i.e. at what point does the victim count the change in their learning, skill, or status as significant); the form with which you will measure (i.e. is it better to use a number, percentage, amount, or rating?); the source of your information (e.g. is the best indicator in program data, from family members, or observable?), and the process of extracting the information from the source (e.g. is it best to review documents, use surveys, conduct face-to-face or telephone interviews, or use a trained observer?). After determining and evaluating your indicators of success and establishing specific measures of the process, your reporting of results should include information about the variables and limitations of your sources, collection processes, timeliness, volume, percentages, and other factors that affect the reliability of your results. Pre- and post-tests are particularly instructive, however not possible in most crisis and minimal contact cases. Accurate indicators of outcome attainment increase accountability of advocates and partners, and allow Victim Advocates to focus their passion on activities that are linked to improvements in victims' lives.

Chapter 6
Applying Outcomes Internally
The end of learning is doing

How has the culture of victim services changed?

The emphasis in the 1980's was outputs—how many people can you serve? During the 1990's the challenge was efficiency—what is your cost per client or service? Today the focus is on outcomes—are your efforts making a difference in victims' lives? None of the output, efficiency, or outcome questions are going away, so program resources are critical to managing each emphasis.

Improving outcomes is a neverending task. Our aim is for the revolution of victim outcomes to become embedded in the values and principles of our field's culture. Toward that end, we must weave victim outcomes into the fabric of what we do and what we measure.   Evaluations are not just burdensome grant requirements to answer external questions of viability and compliance. They measure proximity to the vision and missions of our agencies, which is why the cliché exists: "You count what you care about."

> *Our aim is for the revolution of victim outcomes to become embedded in the values and principles of our field's culture.*

Dr. Michael Patton, a leader in the evaluation field, notes, "Changing your thinking about the vision for evaluation is actually useful in setting up a culture of practice, involving the leaders in the organization, modeling evaluation use. It means spending staff meeting time on evaluation issues, monitoring evaluations, dialoguing about them, thinking about them, and considering their consequences. It is not about moving that thing off your desk as fast as possible, and delegating it down to lower levels in the organization" (Patton, uic.edu, 2/14/08).

Evaluating success based on victim outcomes rather than the delivery of a service or support means creating systems to be responsive to people. The goal is not to evaluate and report, but to monitor and manage. Implementing victim-driven outcomes involves improving responsiveness and effectiveness for victims at all levels of the organization (Lampkin, Morley, 2004).

One of the ongoing problems to which there is a plethora of solutions is how to create an organizational culture of quality that results in consist-

**Top 5 Internal
Uses of Outcomes**

• Staff recruiting and hiring

• Staff focus and teamwork

• Guide budgets and justify expenses

• Improve service delivery and program structure

• Guide organizational change and planning with mission alignment

ently high quality services. At least part of the answer is to swallow the mission statement whole and apply it in as many facets of the organization as possible—both internally and externally.

What are the internal uses of outcomes?

Developing an outcome-oriented culture begins prior to the task of training staff and volunteers. Advertising for staff and marketing for volunteers is about catching the hearts of those dedicated to helping people. For example, employment advertisements could list the key outcomes the position will accomplish in changing victims' lives, rather than listing job description tasks. Ads should focus on candidates' willingness and ability to help victims. For example, write applications and conduct interviews according to outcome categories. Relate tasks and activities in job descriptions to specific outcomes for the board of directors, interns, staff, and community volunteers. Linking outcome-based activities with peoples' strengths may help narrow the applications to those who demonstrate uniquely desired abilities. When filling positions, consider the strengths an applicant must have to attain particular goals or outcomes in a logic model:

   a. Is more independence or teamwork needed (e.g. lone program coordinator versus a team of court Victim Advocates)?

   b. Are short- or long-term relationship skills required (e.g. multi-tasking shelter management versus in-depth relationships with victims of severe violence)?

   c. Are emotional and intuitive skills or deductive and academic understandings preferred (e.g. crisis line listening skills versus complex systems explanations of the justice system)?

   d. Are listening or speaking skills most helpful (e.g. understanding personal victim needs in spite of odd behaviors/situations versus an articulate speaker to communicate an outcome matrix and success stories to grantors)?

Focus on applicants' strengths

Staff Recruiting and Hiring

• Link outcomes in job ads for all positions

• Interview questions can reflect outcome goals

• Match talents, skills, and values with position

• Quality staff want to do something valuable

• Roleplay job situations related to outcomes

There are many interviewing techniques and styles. One option is to distinguish applicants' strengths, and then align strengths with position responsibilities. People have natural gifts and strengths with which they are born. These abilities and personal qualities can be improved and developed, but they are innate. This includes some people's preference for task jobs such as the natural tendency toward mathematical and formulaic thinking. Some nonconfrontational Victim Advocates may be especially good at customer service and less capable of advocating for changes and victim rights within the justice system. Some people are particularly suited for administrative positions because of their ability to think conceptually and strategically.

Some skills and talents are acquired through education and experience. People learn these specializations over time with practice and training, such as learning data management software or common responses to grief or victimization. Testing for these learned retention skills is possible, and more likely to be visible on resumes and applications.

Applicants' future aspirations reveal insights into their life views and values. What talents do they hope to achieve, what positions or responsibilities excite them, and what in life and in the victim advocacy field would they like to do if money were no object?

Use interview skills

Good interviewing skills start with good listening, observation, and analytical skills. The interviewers learn about the candidates by listening, not by talking. An interviewer being friendly and interactive is helpful, but interviews offer precious little time to determine if the candidates will, by innate talents, learned skills, and/or personal values, improve or detract from the mission of reaching victim outcomes. By covering diverse subjects with candidates, there is an increased likelihood of learning about the important strengths a candidate has. This also helps differentiate between the responses that are candid and accurate, and those that are simply angling for approval and a job offer.

The interview process is valuable for orienting and evaluating potential staff on victim outcomes. Having candidates roleplay their responses to victims in traumatic moments regarding their particular safety, healing, justice, and financial well-being can illustrate the candidates' abilities. It also models the agency's ideals that success is measured by improvements in victims' lives. The program's focus on making a difference in victims' lives may inspire applicants to catch the same vision and passion. The cream of the applicant crop is anyone looking for a place to make a difference with their work, not just pay the bills and have a decent work environment.

Match activities with personalities

Beyond attempting to match the skills and personalities of candidates to outcome-related tasks, activities need to be matched with candidates. For example, positions handling communications, task forces, protocol development, and public policy issues will need writing, verbal, and project management skills, as well as interpersonal wisdom. Overall, it is important that the candidates remain grounded in the true goal of all Victim Advocate jobs—assuring a tangible benefit in victims' safety, healing, justice,

---

Staff Recruiting and Hiring

Outcomes and correlated activities dictate strength, skill, and experience needed

- Coalition building requires project management
- Crisis counseling requires social work
- Volunteer management requires sales orientation

Interview for Advocate differences

- Personal vs. system advocacy
- Short- vs. long-term advocacy
- Written vs. verbal advocacy

and financial recovery.

Good therapists, crisis counselors, group leaders, intake specialists, and shelter case managers usually enjoy the stories of people's lives. This orientation to people is critical to reading between the lines and finding victims' unique needs and strengths. Having staff who can build on victims' strengths rather than focus on minimizing their weaknesses is vital since the most critical building block for long-term healing is for victims to believe in themselves.

Volunteer coordinators and fundraisers must be self-directed and self-motivated since these positions require salesperson-like abilities. Both positions must correlate to victim outcomes, but the position goals are more operation-related for such items as volunteer hours, tasks, quality, and longevity. This special set of skills uses different best practices than most personnel managers. For example, one of the strengths needed is the ability to build relationships and trust with those who donate time and money, while understanding that the key relationships are between the donors and the victims benefiting from their generosity and compassion. In other words, they must be able to foster the volunteers' commitment to the victims served, not to the volunteer programs or coordinators.

Some Victim Advocate positions are task-oriented and may need stronger organizational abilities, innate list-making tendencies, inclinations toward routine, and the ability to follow bureaucratic instructions without excessive frustration. A natural desire to nail down loose ends before considering a task complete is also beneficial while working through the recurring hurdles of agency and justice systems.

Testing applicant aptitudes, strengths, abilities, and understanding of success as being client-driven can position future employees for success. Evaluating and interviewing candidates are talents that insight and experience can improve, and are important in finding volunteers and staff that in turn reach outcomes.

Know the victims' needs

We have all been to restaurants in which the server appears to have a photographic memory of each item on the menu and how they are cooked and seasoned. Should not the Victim Advocate "servers" similarly know the options for meeting victims' initial needs? If core needs are not internalized, omissions and errors by Advocates will be the result when trying to respond with essential services and options.

Staff Focus and Team Work

- Know the customer menu (victim outcomes)

- Highlight victims' stories with outcome quotes

- Focus staff reports on outcomes

- Integrate outcomes into all staff training

- Prioritize outcomes in staff meetings and on bulletin boards and posters

- Train all staff on how to answer the question "What do you do?" with outcomes (helping victims starts with the first contact)

Focus the goals of meetings

Meetings outside the agency must correlate to specific victim or program outcomes. Do meetings with businesses, social services, and government entities closely relate to a victim outcome or activity? Similarly, membership dues, reports, and ongoing community partnerships must also relate to victim outcomes. Some activities may need to be included for ancillary benefits, such as educational efforts for the public and justice officials. In that case, an educational logic model should be created to focus the activities and to link them with victim outcomes.

Promote successes

Retention of victim advocacy professionals and volunteers is often due to their commitment to the victim-healing results of the program. Even underpaid staff members are likely to believe in the value of the organization when there is a clear focus on improving victim's lives, not just on increasing outputs. Work environment studies repeatedly report that people are more likely to stay in jobs in which they feel valued, see results, have friendships, and have reasonable compensation. Feeling valued and seeing lives changed are direct outgrowths of attaining and reporting positive outcomes throughout the program. Developing outcome-oriented leadership is a long-term investment in helping victims attain their greatest potential for recovery (Foster, Reinelt, Sullivan, 2002).

Developing outcome-oriented leadership is a long-term investment in helping victims attain their greatest potential for recovery.

Clarify the processes

Clear victim outcomes provide staff not only mission alignment, but also direction, organization, and task clarity. Victim Advocate job routines provide dependability, yet focusing on daily job tasks can also foster misunderstandings about the roles and value of other staff. Perspective on the links within the whole organization usually depends on administrative guidance. Job purposes (why), tasks (what), and methods (how) grow convoluted and unfocused over time, partly from ordinary staff turnover. Outcomes, if linked and emphasized internally, provide the glue to hold tasks, staff, and program direction together.

Subdivide outcomes

The more specific, understandable, and realistic the outcome goal, the more likely it will be achieved. You reach outcomes in stages, and each succeeding level is a goal and a "win" in the process of reaching outcomes in the model. Each position, department, program, staff, and supervisor requires identifiable goals, both clarified and updated. Adding a simple

The more specific, understandable, and realistic the outcome goal, the more likely it will be achieved.

phrase that captures the essence of the goal for each task or position narrows the focus and defines success. The master plan or model illuminates how each position and person is inter-connected and important to improving victims' lives. As the saying goes, "by the yard is hard, inch by inch is a cinch."

Emphasize early needs

Initial outcomes can focus program activities, job descriptions, staff hours, and printed material. Initial outcomes usually have fewer influencing factors, so evaluating attainment is easier. Additionally, initial outcomes can orient the language, content, and style of mailings, fundraisers, and newsletters so the program's mission influences staff, justice officials, and the public. When in doubt, provide the most comprehensive and highest quality services to the earliest and foundational victim needs. Reaching later outcomes requires program and personnel maturation, planning, and, often, special funding.

Link training with outcomes

Selecting the right staff for the right training can be based on enhancing skills and programs relating to outcomes rather than an attraction to vaguely useful and interesting topics. When staff members submit requests for training, they should indicate how the training links to an outcome or related activity. In other words, the staff can note how the requested training will improve any listed activity for that outcome. This training selection tool places the burden on staff to think differently about their training goals, even if the training presenter is not outcome oriented. It is also another way for staff to stay in an outcome culture and continue to reexamine their outcomes and activities.

Training must address the skills relevant to staff's role in attaining a specific outcome, as well as the outcome-oriented knowledge, attitudes, and behaviors that are required to use the skills. Training performance objectives should specifically relate to the desired (or required) outcome skills and knowledge.

Use victims' words

Focusing a victim advocacy program on outcomes includes recognizing that success relates to victim recovery. Quotes from victims are wonderful ways to link outcome concepts to everyday work. Victim stories, if you listen carefully, frequently mention some hurdle crossed or positive feeling related to safety, healing, justice, and financial recovery. Asking staff if they've heard any good comments from victims can elicit victim

Initial outcomes can orient the language, content, and style of mailings, fundraisers, and newsletters so the program's mission influences staff, justice officials, and the public.

Victim stories, if you listen carefully, frequently mention some hurdle crossed or positive feeling related to safety, healing, justice, and financial recovery.

success stories, develop pride, and provide opportunities for spontaneous praise. It takes a team effort to reach victim goals: reception, referrals, correspondence, notices, data management, intake, counseling, case coverage, etc. That synergy is a cause for celebration.

Involve stakeholders

The level of staff and stakeholder involvement in developing and examining outcomes is the key to long-term commitment to outcomes as a service paradigm. Visualizing why the program exists and how it benefits victims is at the core of accomplishing outcomes. Brainstorming as a facilitated group activity can give clarity and guidance to programs, plans, strategies, staff, and help manage and fine tune activities and services. When outcomes are clear and accountability is outcome-specific, there is more room for flexibility in services.

Question results

Even if every victim participates in an outcome evaluation, many variables prohibit the assumption that collected data necessarily reflects the intended and presumed results. For example, victims may interpret questions differently than intended and indicators may not be accurate. Responses may not be given in a neutral environment, and victims may not understand that their answers likely impact programming.

Clarify job descriptions

Besides common legal verbiage, common tasks, and medical requirements to return to work, job descriptions should contain the specific duties and outcomes correlated with each staff position. Setting and reaching outcome measure target percentages and numbers are rarely useful in job descriptions or performance evaluations. It is expensive to confirm statistically that the responses actually reflect all the victims served by one particular individual. Every job description, however, should include quality and outcome purpose statements. Sufficient guides and expectations should also be included so the employee sclearly understand that victim outcomes are the core of the program. A common emphasis on victim outcomes in an organization can have the unintended consequence of blurring and merging job descriptions among support, direct service, and management staff since all are focused on attaining victim priorities. [See Exhibit 6 for a sample job description and performance management form]

Evaluate staff

The management adage, "You count what you care about," also makes

Staff Focus and Team Work

- Common outcomes bring context and value

- Outcomes counter Murphy's Law and randomness

- Outcomes focus staff meetings on the questions, "How are we doing?" and "Why are we doing what we do?"

- Outcomes allow focus on job purpose, tasks, and methods

- Outcomes create feedback and reasons to praise staff

- Outcomes are evaluation criteria: knowledge, collaboration, training, reporting, and commitment

the point that you should include some outcome-related items when evaluating staff performance. There are many styles of evaluation, and a quality and outcome-focused organization must maintain both accountability and a style of learning, discussing, monitoring, and adapting that feeds a culture of quality. A strict top-down and one-sided annual rating process is not usually the ideal method, and not likely to provide the ongoing motivation, praise, and guidance that staff desire. Existing evaluations may be adapted by adding outcomes (see examples below), or by prioritizing outcomes by assigning more weight in the evaluation process or score.

Useful staff evaluation criteria and sample practices regarding outcomes:

1. Outcome Knowledge—Test recall of the victim outcomes and related program outcomes, since the "server" should know the customer "menu." Knowledge of the link between core services and attainment of specific outcomes should also be well-known by direct service staff.

2. Collaboration Effort—Evaluate actions staff took to understand, design, create, maintain, and improve the collaborations needed to improve victim outcomes, both inside and outside the program.

3. Training Effort—Assess staff learning (and teaching) about outcomes by counting the number and evaluating the quality (length, usefulness, correlation, etc.) of educational courses, training notes, books and articles summarized or written, participation in blogs, etc. In essence, has the staff member utilized their personal and professional abilities and resources to learn and/or teach about outcomes?

4. Reporting Effort—Appraise the number, sophistication, and usefulness of staff reports that integrate outcomes. For example, what are the outcome values and knowledge demonstrated in staff and partner meeting reports?

5. Commitment to Innovation—Evaluate what analysis and experimentation has resulted in adapting and creating services that might improve victim outcomes. In other words, if program income depended on victims purchasing services, how would the staff person demonstrate innovative and improved ways of doing business?

    a. Does the staff person suggest new links or services to improve an outcome?

    b. Does the staff person ask, "What benefit would there be in changing this service or procedure?"

    c. Does the staff person alter or scrutinize factors that can influ-

If program income depended on victims purchasing services, how would the staff person demonstrate innovative and improved ways of doing business?

ence victim outcomes?

    d. Does the staff person recommend any new access, structure, or process concepts in order to improve outcomes?

Job descriptions and evaluation tools are part of the culture change of the organization and of staff as they include the four quality areas of access, structure, process, and outcomes. [See Exhibit 6 for a sample executive director job description and assessment tool]

Use staff meetings

Incorporating outcomes into the daily thinking and practices of staff is key to good outcomes and for any hope of improving results. Take time at staff meetings for staff to compliment each other on who has, since the last meeting, ably provided services for a victim need that helped him/her reach an outcome; collaborated to improve systems and community responses to victims; and/or communicated outcomes effectively with victims during assessment, service delivery, or media interviews. In other words, focus on how staff have used outcomes in the context of daily work.

Change agendas

Boards of directors, grantors, and funding sources often evaluate programs by asking financial and structural questions about an organization. The effect is to diminish the priority of program goals, outcomes, and stories of victim advocacy that accomplish the program's mission. To combat this, inject outcomes into program assessments. Stakeholders and supporters should have more information about the true value of services in people's lives. Similarly, collaborative reviews need to focus on the interplay of services and roles of partners as well as measures of success in lives. Victim outcomes are the reasons to raise money, write grants, pay salaries, and donate volunteer hours. Promoting habitual attention to outcomes, measurement tools, influencing factors, and comparisons with prior outcome results, helps maintain focus on the reason the organization exists.

Use resources and reports

Stakeholders also benefit from reporting on outcome-specific expenditures and adjustments in spending to improve outcome results. Spending money to implement more effective service delivery strategies is a high level of outcome integration and demonstrates leadership attention to detail and results. For example, are victims of violent crime receiving state victim compensation funds only in cases involving prosecution? It is legitimate to ask, "Should we shift resources (e.g. staff time) to reach reported but unprosecuted cases to increase victim compensation for more victims?"

Sample stakeholder and media report:

Our agency has made a difference in victims' lives with an additional 21 victims reporting being able to pay their crime-related bills. This is a 30% increase over last year and amounts to a $90,000 increase of crime-related payment of medical expenses, income losses, and other victim debts (such outcome improvements should be augmented by quotes or stories from victims about how their lives improved as a result of them). This was made possible in collaboration with the local police department, which provides a victim rights palm card to each victim it contacts. The state victim's compensation program also reported an increase of 26 victims who filed claims in this jurisdiction compared to last year at this time. This is a 40% increase in claims filed in the county (an output improvement). Our agency's reports are substantiated by a cross check of compensation claims paid that shows 46% of the new compensation requests were victims of unsolved crimes.

The more frequent, varied, and simple the information, the more involved people are in learning activities. The more memorable the story, the faster and longer lasting the learning.

Specifically, a staff assignment can be to research and report monthly on victim fiancial compensation, thus promoting the value of street officers and road patrols informing victims about the funds and other resources given to victims.

Orient staff daily

People learn better with repetition, simplicity, action, and real-world examples. The more frequent, varied, and simple the information, the more involved people are in learning activities. The more memorable the story, the faster and longer lasting the learning. For example:

1. Post a question about how to improve or define an outcome near the employee entrance, sign-in-board, lockers, break room, or similar location. Each week or month post a different outcome question, along with the answer or update from the prior posting.

2. Use skill-building exercises to show the value of victim outcomes with activities and games in staff meetings. Use, perhaps, an "unfair" game to help staff relate to the victim's frustration and the predicament of unreliable court schedules and decisions. For example, instruct staff that the goal is to reach the other side of the room across a grid of taped squares on the floor numbered from 1 to 25 (five by five). Unknown to the players, the referee occasionally changes the rules on which squares are land mines that send the staff member back to the end of the line (sometimes the referee apologizes when caught but other times seems offended). Players (victims) initially believe the system (grid, landmines, and referee) are logical and dependable, but over time, they notice other players being treated differently and given different information. They increasingly wonder if the problem is their memory, knowledge of the rules, or referee favoritism that makes success difficult, and they grow irritated as the supposed five minute game takes 20 minutes and cuts into lunch break.

3. Ask (with caution and sensitivity) an articulate victim to recount their travails through the justice system for the staff. This can remind staff how unprepared victims are for the language and process of the justice system, and how this causes anxiety and confusion—even though they might have had a good experience with a Victim Advocate. Take note of victim impact statements that demonstrate how the system, not the criminal, can negatively affect and re-victimize survivors.

4. Roleplay with staff the common victim difficulties in reaching outcomes. For example, have each staff member alternate as a victim

describing their frustrating obstacles, and then have each take their turn as the responding Victim Advocate until all have participated. Obstacles that the role playing staff member must respond to may be serious or humorous, but in the end reminds players that victim outcomes are not accomplished in a vacuum, and victimizations always come for victims in the middle of ongoing workplace issues, personal relationship problems, illnesses, car repairs, weather emergencies, military deployments, school events, appointments, etc.

5. Question staff on which activities logically connect with particular outcomes. This increases general awareness of why certain activities are valued and may lead to discussion about the imperfect connections due to influencing factors. The discussion may elicit comments about the need to be more aware, skilled, knowledgeable, or have better listening skills and open-minded attitudes from Victim Advocates to address victims' particular needs. For example, talking about victim compensation may be the wrong action when the victim displays emotional needs for support and wants to feel believed and affirmed, but it is the correct action when a medical bill needs to be paid.

Use an Activity Manual

A useful tool for Victim Advocates is an activity manual. It helps them (and victims) know what steps and actions may help meet specific needs and outcomes (U.S. Department of Justice, Sexual Assault Advocate/Counselor Training, 2008). This might appear to complicate advocacy by adding service options and considerations. Actually it simplifies the process of helping reach victim outcomes by clarifying what actions are connected and logical. An activity manual is a road map with clear steps to help avoid distractions on the path to the outcome desired by the victim.

An activity manual is an outcome task and topic cheat sheet. [See Exhibit 7] It provides Victim Advocates a resource for quick reference and insight to help them meet victims' needs—both those known by the victim, and those not yet considered. Items for reference include common techniques, collaboration options, referral possibilities, and ideas for those rare shot-in-the-dark advocacy opportunities. Ideally, this quick resource guide is adapted for local use by adding phone numbers, counselor referrals, etc. For example, in the activity manual, options for responses to victims reporting financial losses (e.g. theft of a stolen wallet or purse) include a list of updated toll-free contact information, office hours, and replacement costs for credit cards, driver's licenses, birth certificates, library cards, etc. The list is also helpful to other property and violent crime victims who

Itemize options for every outcome in the activity manual

- Creating a safety assessment and plan
- Providing a 911 cell phone
- Helping with protection orders
- Providing a list of contacts and costs for replacing important documents
- Providing emergency contacts for missing children, bomb threats, and identity theft

lose information. It can be reviewed by phone, on a web site, e-mailed, or mailed to the victim.

The activity manual can also list common trauma symptoms and initial Victim Advocate responses. This reminds Advocates of the range of emotions that ought to be explored with victims to help them reach the outcome of decreased crime-related symptoms (Victims of Crime - A Social Work Response, 2006). With the list of trauma symptoms should be a list of prompts for Advocates' responses to possible trauma emotions such as fear, extreme anger, loneliness, and feeling out of control, as well as prompts to respond to behaviors such as nightmares, flashbacks, self-blame, and inability to do routine tasks. A short list can be provided for reference between phone calls, while more in-depth information could be used for training or self-study when preparation time is available. [See Exhibit 7a for suggested responses to traumatic emotions]

Update lists

Maintaining up-to-date resources provides fingertip access for victims and Victim Advocates. For example, keep a list of specialized counselors for different types of crime victims, as well as locations and costs to test for sexually transmitted diseases. Self-help libraries and website resource lists should be included as references in an activity manual that links services to specific outcomes, and can provide simplicity for victims.

Internal Outcome Uses for Guiding Budgets and Expenses

Budgeting is more than resource allocation. It is part of the process of providing quality services that help victims reach their outcomes. Creating good budgets demands a balance between a focus on money and on mission, since neither can exist without the other. Managing the budget efficiently helps Victim Advocates provide the most effective services with the least amount of cost.

Decide the question

There are two primary budget questions. What are the critical needs of victims that you can significantly affect? How can you provide comprehensive and high quality services that address those important needs in the most cost effective manner? A logic model is useful in writing grants, planning budgets, and in developing organizational strategies to determine victims' problems, how to address them, and whether your services actually reduce or eliminate the problems. [See Exhibits 8 and 8a for sample logic models]

Guide Budgets and Expenses

- Budgeting is part of the outcome process
- Personnel costs are highest, so
  - Link staff with outcomes
  - Correlate staff hours to results
  - Adjust staff pay by value to outcomes
- Grants are for outcomes, not vice versa
- Dues, memberships, trainings, and office spaces must correlate with outcomes

Evaluate personnel costs carefully

The largest portions of victim advocacy budgets are personnel-related, so staffing levels, pay scales, and benefit packages are significant factors in budgeting. Even staff with good work ethics, effective and efficient strategies, and clear goals may still not be doing the activities linked to attaining victim outcomes.

Value efficiency

The capstone for managers is the ability to persistently monitor and adapt operations, services, and structural costs for efficiency. It is harder to simplify the already complex than it is to add components or ideas until the system becomes complex. Efficiency is a measure of quality, but analyzing efficiency is problematic for many reasons. For example, personalities and styles of advocacy vary among even expert Victim Advocates. Advocates can be particularly capable and efficient in one area and not another. In addition, caseloads and needs of victims usually vary, even for the same victim from day to day. Furthermore, carefully appropriating hours takes time and study, and accomplishing major realignments of programs and staff assignments is also inefficient.

Efficiency is important. Taking time to strategize with staff on creating or improving services for unserved victims, unmet victim needs, and poor outcome results is an opportunity that can result in positive group dynamics and results. The extra cost for retreat time to brainstorm options and expenses is often justified with the improved efficiency and value of services that follow.

An accurate and fully utilized outcome logic model with linked services is the gold standard for both results and efficiency, but it is not the whole story. Such a model does not indicate quality and efficiency, for example, if electricity is being wasted by clogged air conditioner filters, inefficient light bulbs, or using preset high ink-usage levels on office printers rather than "draft" or "quick print" settings. The stories flooding the media about companies "going green" are equally applicable to victim service organizations. Financial efficiencies can be monitored as part of the master plan by adding a column or box next to the activity or outcome in the model for tracking the efficiencies or earth-friendly progress for staffing, volunteer program, vehicles, facility space, etc.

Do something

Budget and outcome correlations are more subjective than objective. However, a determined effort to address those links can only enhance the

---

Guide Budgets and Expenses

- Agree on outcome priorities (e.g. court advocacy vs. individual counseling)

- Discern which staff and partners influence which outcomes by what percentage

- Exercise caution in calculating future estimates based on past performance

- Be careful when matching budget timeframes with outcome timeframes

change in culture and improve the chances that spending money will result in victim outcomes. Some effort is better than no effort, even if the benefit of the time invested is not immediately obvious.

Remember quality factors

Some budget issues do not directly link to outcomes. Rather, they link to quality access, structure, and process issues. For example, having cash flow to avoid repeated borrowing of money (e.g. for grants paying on a reimbursement basis) does not improve an outcome, but is a necessary part of a cost-effective organizational structure.

Similarly, the value of institutional memory and expertise of long-term staff is difficult to prioritize. Though retaining staff can become expensive, it may be worth its value in attaining victim outcomes. Juggling costs to update equipment (structure) and maintaining welcoming furnishings (process) are subjective values requiring choices when funds are limited. There are efficiency and long-term cost trade-offs to consider when staff must wait to use a common printer or copier, endure a slow computer server constantly delaying the data management system, or burn out as a result of having insufficient on-call staff.

Consider time frame

Linking budget decisions and outcomes can be problematic due to different grant periods. Budget-making tends to be an annual event. However, outcomes can be shorter term or perhaps measured only years later. Similarly, budgets are guesses about the future year or particular period, and outcomes measure past data. It is not always clear how to overlay future spending with past data.

Keep data current

Collecting and evaluating data is an ongoing process. It is critical that budget decisions reflect information that is accurate to a reasonable degree of confidence. When looking at outcomes that do not reflect early and initial needs, the imprecision of indicators and other influencing factors requires many months of collection and analysis before that information can be used to adjust budgets.

Cut small first

Program managers who deal with fluctuating grants or local government budget cuts are familiar with the painful experience of reducing expenses. Sometimes budget cuts just six months after the introduction of a new program or service seem disproportionate to perceived problems, so small cuts done incrementally are better than early sweeping cuts. The fewer changes to the links between budget expenses and outcome attainment, the better. Examples of smaller budget efficiency adjustments may include: eliminating lease costs of postage machines, reducing staff development and vehicle use or rentals, reducing custodial help by a day or two per week (e.g. with attention to food garbage on off-days), and cutting resource material.

Larger cuts with greater impact on services could include reducing building space, staff on-call costs, staff hours, and positions. Creative staff can often help find cheaper alternatives to accomplishing outcome activities or efficiencies when asked to participate in cost cutting.

Reconsider core issues

One financial evaluation test is to ask staff efficiency questions regarding the cost of what they actually accomplish, in either outputs or outcomes. Ask for opinions on the likelihood of particular activities achieving positive outcomes. In this process, ask staff and stakeholders about financial factors, such as:

1. Routine assumptions (e.g. What value to victims or the organization are particular expense items and levels?)
2. Past choices (e.g. Which activities are now prioritized and what options were eliminated?)
3. Assigned values (e.g. Should more victim outcomes be addressed? Are some services more important because the trauma of victims is so great? Is the service delivery and partnership process too complex or not creative enough?)
4. Budget feeling (e.g. Do the budget categories and direction feel reasonable and acceptable?)
5. Possible harm (e.g. How difficult will the budget change be to victims, partners, staff, and the ongoing marketing of the mission to the public?)
6. Destructive change (e.g. Is the cost and disruption caused by the change worth the shift or reduction in resources?)

Keep records

Keeping the written record is important for future decision-making and program reviews in order to avoid "reinventing the wheel". An evaluation of expenses can also supply ammunition for a recommendation to increase staff pay and education requirements, or beef up a position to increase the likelihood of a particular outcome attainment.

Compare and Improve Programs and Service Strategies

- There are 10,000 victim assistance programs in the U.S.
- Take time to search websites and bulletin boards
- Compare to state and national benchmarks
- Improve, realign, and redesign program and delivery
- Note program differences—structure, activity, and types of cases

Internal outcome uses in comparing and improving programs and service strategies (micro adjustments)

Increasing numbers of victim advocacy programs are developing outcomes and measures in response to private sector grant requirements, United Way allocations procedures, and demand from state and federal grantors for performance-based measures. State and national certification and accreditation bodies also require more than client satisfaction measures, enveloping numerous private nonprofit victim service programs such as rape crisis centers and domestic violence shelters. [Visit the Office for Victims of Crime at the U.S. Department of Justice, www.ovcttac.gov/taresources/straPlan.cfm, for a Strategic Planning Toolkit]

Compare results

The trend of programs comparing victim outcome results internally and externally also provides growing opportunities for research and comparison between indicators, data collection sources and methods, as well as resulting data (Cowan, Hatry, & Hendricks, 2004). Additionally, outcome comparison data can increase the complexity and accuracy of understanding victim needs.

Comparing data and outcomes is insightful and instructive, but victim services that appear similar can have significantly different variables and influencing factors, as can individual victims. Even differences in environment, culture, and community values can influence results of otherwise similar services in two different jurisdictions. Variables also include staff size, number of victims assisted, types of victim assistance, geographic coverage, partnership linkages, residential vs. office programs, gender, family involvement, and victimization complexity. Other examples of program comparison issues involve service differences, length and content of victim advocacy hours with victims, and the number of services utilized and noted to be beneficial to victims. Collecting and recording of data procedures may also require evaluation to determine if outcome data is comparable. For example, changes in survey wording or collection processes influence the results reported.

Revise Victim Impact Statements

If the four outcomes of safety, healing, justice, and restitution are the primary need areas of victims, then they are the logical components for victims to communicate concerns regarding fear, feelings, fairness, and financial reimbursement. Victim impact statements must include the four areas of victim needs: safety, healing, justice, and financial restitution. [See Chapter 4 for detailed explanations]

Compare and Improve Programs and Service Strategies

- Evaluate jobs, hours, and materials
- Diagram activities to outcomes
- Focus Victim Impact Statements on victims' safety, healing, justice, and restitution

Compare and Improve Programs and Service Strategies

- Tracking data likely shows logic model gaps
- Stakeholder participation is important
- Signs of success or necessary improvements
  - Activities expanded or modified due to lacking correlation
  - New barriers or influencing factors
  - New victims or demographics

Be creative and brave

The art of intelligent and curious questioning of variables and likely linkages can result in valuable service changes, which in turn result in significant victim improvements. Interpreting data can tease out variables, barriers, and influencing factors that haven't been considered. This often leads to ideas and discoveries that may influence decisions about services, marketing, or other access, structure, process, or outcome improvements. Much like efficiency is the capstone for quality management, the effective connection of outcomes, activities, and other relevant factors is the capstone for victim advocacy advancement.

Internal Outcome uses in realigning and redesigning programs (macro direction)

Outcomes are both processes and goals (Carden, Earl, & Smutylo, 2001). Just as the areas of access, structure, and process are reducible into layers and sub-levels, so are outcomes. Besides the use of activity manuals noted earlier, other proactive designs can promote cultural change toward a victim-focused organization. One of the keys to determining an organization's future—its strategic plan—depends on knowing its intended outcomes, its mission. Outcomes are the reason your programs exist and must be clear before you strategize activities, services, resources, and particular focus areas (Barry, 1997). Outcomes are key guides in your strategic planning process (Strategic Planning Toolkit, 2008).

Require reporting

Some of the ways to integrate outcomes into daily activities, forms, and procedures are to require all board, annual, and staff reports to include outcome data and activities. The program's definition of success must include not only the statistical outcome data from victim surveys, but also the peripheral indicators of success such as victim cards, e-mails, and comments. For example, a victim statement, "I wouldn't be alive today if it weren't for you," is indicative of a safety outcome success.

Write a brief and clear mission statement

A fundamental starting point in achieving successful outcomes is to have outcome-based program and agency mission statements. The visionary goal of outcomes can be woven into mission statements, newsletter content, websites, organization logos, and marketing materials. If reaching outcomes is why the organization exists, everything connects to outcomes. The mission statement is a public sound-byte that explains why victims

---

Guide Agency Direction

- Focus on access, structure, process and outcomes (plus efficiency and effectiveness)
- Employ strategic planning, mergers, and agency designs
  - Use board and annual reports
  - Base the program's concept of success on outcomes
  - Create and evaluate new services

Guide Agency Direction

- Reflect outcomes in a mission statement
- Create an outcome based vision statement and logo
- Identify policy and legislative changes
- Coordinate committees, taskforces, board members, grants, protocols, newsletters, website designs, and research

Outcomes keep your mission in touch with reality!

Guide Agency Direction

- Outcome measures are snapshots in time
- Long-term tracking is necessary for longitudinal view
- Record dates of important changes
  - Staff member changes
  - Staffing levels and duties
  - New protocols, procedures, and policies
  - Revised surveys and interview procedures

need the organization. The face of the organization, the logo, must also embrace the concept or feeling of outcomes as the organization's priority.

Affect public policy

An outcome-focused organization will have, as a priority, staff and resources invested to affect change through legislation and public policy. These types of internal decisions can be just as critical in attaining outcomes as hiring new staff or writing new grants. For example, in some states, criminal restitution payments are not mandatory in the law, and to make matters worse, judges routinely order their own court costs paid before the victims receive *their* money and *their* justice from the offenders' fined money. In such situations, the offenders may be attempting to make the victims whole financially, but are hindered by the justice system itself. The offenders think they are paying the victims, and the victims think they will receive that repayment, but instead the court siphons off those precious healing and restorative justice dollars meant for victims, to pay court expenses. Public policy decisions can impact and resolve injustices for victims and offenders.

Monitor trends

Outcome improvement changes are important to track, document, and evaluate continuously in order for adaptations to be useful. For example, staff turnover affects outcome knowledge and service expertise. New collaborations, new victim rights legislation or court decisions, and other influencing factors may correlate to outcome improvements or reductions.

Be patient

Many external or internal strategy changes will take time to impact outcome indicators and measures. If the numbers of applications remain steady, for example, but payments to victims significantly drop, then the influencing factors need to be reexamined. Possibly police officers are providing fewer applications or are giving inaccurate explanations. Maybe administrative forms or procedures in the victim compensation program have reduced user-friendliness, or maybe an increase in criminal restitution or insurance payments simply resulted in reduced eligibility or need for funds. These types of factors should be taken into consideration.

Outcomes provide the parameters to guide both intra-agency and inter-agency decisions. Not only do people naturally seek routines in their personal and professional lives, they also have natural impulses to associate with their peers and familiar professionals. These tendencies toward routines are yet more reasons for leaders to refocus and reinvigorate outcomes as the core for all decisions.

Chapter 6 Summary: Applying Outcomes Internally

Understanding and adopting victim outcome logic models and goals are the guiding lights to orient staff members to translate outcomes into everyday actions. How you frame your help wanted ads and interview applicants begins the process of shaping your agency culture. Like a restaurant server knowing the menu, an early goal in nurturing victim advocacy is to inspire and require staff to be intimately familiar with the needs particular to your victims and their initial outcome goals. Individual job descriptions, culture-creating work environments, activities (instruction) manuals, staff meetings content, and governance board agendas should center on your core outcomes. Similarly, staff evaluations can target knowledge, collaboration, training, reporting, and commitment to victim outcomes. Orient your grants and prioritizing your expenses with a focus on outcomes to further indoctrinate all staff and partners. Refocus expenses on tasks and personnel that most improve your ability to reach victim needs, recognizing the limitations of your change theory, time frames, and data accuracy. Adjust and improve programs with discussions, decisions, and comparison to similar program outcomes. Fine-tune the link between outcomes and services as you monitor your success at outcome attainment. Your outcome orientation is the plumb-line for strategic planning, public policy, partnership priorities, and the hub for comprehensive mission alignment.

What you know about outcomes is only as valuable as their integration into the fabric and culture of your organization.

Chapter 7

Applying Outcomes Externally

We're all in this boat together

Five external uses of outcomes

Identifying, focusing, and enhancing stakeholders

Your outcomes define you to the world. With society's fast pace and inclination toward paying attention in bits and bytes, outcome goals remain an organization's steady beacon. Outcomes can tell your story in many ways to a variety of audiences.

People want to join successful organizations as employees, volunteers, and donors. A consistent organizational message of meeting victims' needs is an attractive incentive for people to look twice at your program and join your mission. Involving stakeholders throughout the development, provision, and implementation of services requires planning together, sharing data collected, and reporting mutual outcomes. The methods of communicating the mission may include poetry, graphics, photography, cartoons, drama, audio, and video communication.

Outcomes guide the strategic planning, funding submissions, and goals for events and programs. Having outcomes in place reduces time spent in the initial phases of strategic planning which answer the questions, "Why are we here?" and "Where are we going?" With outcomes providing the mission alignment, you can move more quickly from strategic planning to answer the questions:

1. How are we doing?
2. What must change?
3. How will we achieve those changes?
4. What implementation strategies do we use?

While discussing and designing tasks, contracts, and plans with partners, victim and program outcomes can be the central themes that emanate from the agreements. Some obvious advantages to having clear outcomes are their usefulness in screening and prioritizing new programs and collaborations, guiding grant writing, formulating problem statements and goals, and determining the service delivery sections of contracts. Dovetailing outcomes results in a seamless partnership for the customer's benefit.

Top 5 External Uses of Outcomes

- Identify, focus, and enhance stakeholders
- Attract unreached victims
- Attract funding
- Communicate results to improve public image
- Guide education and prevention efforts

Identify, Focus, and Enhance Stakeholders

- Why you hold fundraisers and give awards
- How you define quality and success
- What you are measured against
- The focus of interagency agreements
- How you design advisory boards

One way to demonstrate the coordination of outcomes and activities with partners is to create a single outcome model with each partner using different colors to denote responsibilities. The inter-connected overlay of the model distinguishes tasks and providers while linking partners with outcomes.

Outcomes with linked measures and activities are most meaningful for determining common points of interests with outcomes (safety healing, justice, and financial stability) with collaborating partner outcomes. Some examples of joint marketing of outcomes with referral sources include:

1. For a church or place of worship, link initial healing outcomes with core expressions of faith, such as, "God cares and so do we—you aren't alone." Then add a tag line with your agency name and phone number.

2. For a mental health facility, link outcomes in an outreach message, such as, "We will believe you" or "We know crime is traumatic" (feeling believed and improving trauma understanding are initial outcomes).

3. For a law enforcement agency, link their interest in victims/witnesses with your justice outcomes, such as promoting "reverse Miranda" victim's rights palm cards for officers to give crime victims, or event themes, such as, "Without victims reporting and testifying, criminals cannot be held accountable."

Attracting unreached victims and referrals

A customer-oriented (victim) marketing strategy is about telling victim success stories. Informing the public about services can be more appealing when victims talk candidly about how they benefited and clearly experienced personal improvements. Reporting that a program is helping more victims or is receiving more grant dollars may be reassuring to some people, but hearing the quality of results from victims is critical. Just as businesses boast about their ability to improve your life with their products, victims want to know that you are improving their lives in specific areas like feeling safer, reducing trauma, having respectful experiences with the justice system, and payment of crime-related bills (Witness Justice, 2008).

Since initial victim outcomes reflect the most likely needs of victims, the words and concepts of those outcomes are key introductory portals to attracting victim attention. Initial correspondence can explain the problems that services address by using quotes from past victims:

1. "I don't feel safe in my own house" (safety).
2. "I can't get over the feeling that something is going to happen" (safety).
3. "I feel violated" (healing).
4. "You can't understand unless you've been through it" (healing).

Attract Unreached Victims

- Market victim service solutions in victims' own words
  - Stories of need
  - Phrases
  - Stories of success
  - Faces and circumstances
  - Direct endorsements

5. "I can't get it out of my head" (healing).
6. "I felt treated like the criminal" (justice).
7. "It's all about me but without me" (justice).
8. "Crime doesn't pay. I do" (restitution).

Sensitive language from staff on important victim issues helps convey an understanding that victims are not alone, support is available, security issues are a priority, financial problems are presumed, and services are focused on their needs.

Where possible, the fastest and cheapest way to market your outcome successes to potential customers (victims who do not know about you or have not called) is to use public service announcements (PSAs), such as free ones available from the United States Department of Justice. A local tag line can be added at the end with your contact information. Professionally produced PSAs, using personal appearances and attestations of victims with local facts and locations are even better tools to catch public attention.

Outcomes tell your story. If you do a good job but do not serve all the victims possible, then many victims are still suffering. Victims must know you can make a difference in their lives, donors need assurance you will use their money wisely, and the public must be convinced you are available and expert in victim services.

Positive outcome results help you explain in simple and understandable terms what you accomplish every day. Fundraising for victim services is similar to raising money for other causes. One key theme is that people give to people, not to causes. Making a difference in someone's life and having that person tell their story is a great message delivered by a great messenger. In addition, allowing victims to use their own words without scripting often adds authenticity and believability.

Attracting funding

There are thousands of tax-exempt organizations in the United States. Most seek funds. Funding sources want to know whom you are helping and if you are making a difference. Outcomes provide anecdotal and statistical accountability. An integrated logic model with clear outcomes is a successful nonprofit business plan.

The best outcomes to use for reporting are the most easily understood and those that influenced initial victim successes. They are foundational for victim improvements in intermediate and later outcome areas of physical, emotional, and financial need.

"Giving a family a fish to eat provides food for today, but teaching them how to fish feeds them forever." This saying is true for victim advocacy as well. Victim advocacy is not just a nice add-on, but it is a critical

Attract Funding with Results

- List fundable work tied to resulting and measureable outcomes
- Match funding sources with bundled activities
  - Civic club focus on children—bundled child-related activities from all initial outcomes
  - Procecution—helped witnesses
  - Law Enforcement—increased reporting
  - Mental health—reduced trauma

Attract Funding with Results

- Use stories of victim outcomes—people give to people, not statistics
- Note that prevention does not replace victim intervention
- Distinguish outputs and outcomes positively
  - Report output volume plus outcomes of changed lives
  - Correlate activities resulting in outcomes
- Report initial outcomes—they reflect immediate needs and are foundational to long-term outcomes

service for victims to improve their feelings of isolation, financial debt, and their ongoing sense of insecurity.

Sometimes donors ask the pejorative question, "Why shouldn't we fund prevention services instead of victim advocacy?" Just about any answer to this question requires tangible outcome measures. Demonstrating results supports positive initial outcomes that are comparable to, for example, quality hospital emergency room services. Ask in response: "Would you advise closing down emergency room services to invest that money into preventing injuries, or should we ensure quality emergency response while we implement prevention services?"

In fact, victim advocacy prevents crime. Who calls 911? Victims call emergency numbers to report and then testify about crime. Without victims' willingness to report and testify, lawbreakers cannot be held accountable. A culture of chaos, indifference, and anonymity breeds irresponsibility and crime. Criminals held accountable result in fewer future crime victims from those offenders.

A follow-up question about the need for victim services is, "Do we want the people who voluntarily report and testify about crime to have no right to be informed, present, heard, safe, or reimbursed?" Callers to 911 are not getting cash rewards. Society, not just victims, has self-interest in holding offenders accountable.

Victim advocacy is also a good investment because, "someday it could be you." Describing outcomes in a few words or a short phrase focuses on the people benefiting from the program and their changed lives. Donors and the public can be reminded that the likelihood of crime means the traumatized and benefited lives could someday be their own.

A similar balance exists for both funding sources and program directors. Both want to address victims' initial outcomes, which are more attainable and measurable, while still having those outcomes logically linked to intermediate outcomes that are in the realm of the programs' influence. Programs should not focus on outcomes that are grandiose and unattainable, but rather adopt secondary (intermediate) outcomes that specifically link to initial outcomes. Goals such as world peace or ending crime are not inspiring to most funders because they are unreasonable. On the other hand, long-term outcomes should be realistic goals desired by victims.

Outcomes for domestic violence victims are good examples of long-term goals. Immediately following their abuse, victims often say, "I just want it to stop." This heartfelt desire is the long-term outcome of domestic violence intervention and prevention services. A temporary or transitional shelter may be an initial outcome and an immediate service. However, the offender could still shoot at, crash into, or otherwise penetrate the shelter's walls regardless of protective actions by staff. Nonviolent living conditions for victims are not fully under the control of advocacy programs, and staying in domestic violence shelters is not 100% safe. The difference between attaining initial and long-term outcomes in victim advocacy depends on victim choices and influencing factors. A shelter may be 98% safe, and the ability of services to stop the violence may be only a 20% influence. The plea, "I just want it to stop," from stalking and domestic violence victims is not just a reasonable goal and outcome to strive for, it is a requirement.

Initial activities should lead to attaining outcomes that lay a foundation for future outcomes. Clearly linking initial outcomes with progress toward intermediate and long-term outcomes is like the connection between giving fish away (emergency advocacy) and teaching victims to fish (long-term improvement in abilities, conditions, etc.). Having a master plan with short- and long-term goals is attractive to funding sources looking for thorough plans that address the safety and recovery of victims. If the master plan is well developed, it can demonstrate activity, outcome, and budget linkages from initial and long-term services. It is then possible to extrapolate costs for budgeting, grant writing, and provide efficiency estimates.

Funding sources usually have special interests or limitations on funding uses. An outcome and activity master plan permits easier bundling of common issues, types of victims, and strategies. For example, applying to a funding source focused on children can include outcomes for all child-related links, such as children witnessing violence, children being sponsored for summer camps, and children provided court orientation and witness assistance, to name a few.

Communicating results and image

You talk about what you care about. This is not only true in our personal lives, but in professional communication as well. Instead of prioritizing the outputs of the program, explain how the volume of work is resulting in measurable improvements (outcomes) in victims' attitudes and knowledge, modified behavior, improved conditions, altered status, or increased skills or insights. A benefit of focusing on outcomes is the ability to publicize the hard work and translate the valuable program tasks into the resulting change for a victim. Tracking outputs (e.g. number of crisis line calls, emergency cell phones provided, or number of victims assisted) are critical pieces of information, but now they connect to clear improvements in the victims' world.

A consistent message across all public forums promotes memory recall

Guide Education and Prevention Efforts

Relate outputs to outcomes

- Transitional housing = Immediate security

- Crisis line calls = Victims feel believed, not alone

- Emergency meals = Financial needs met

- Cell phones given = Immediate security

- Support groups = Life choices made

- Case assistance = Choices in the system

- Victim brochures = Better understanding

- Survivors counseled = Feeling not alone

> **"Everywhere you go, at every conceivable opportunity, reaffirm, reassert, and remind everyone of the basic principles upon which your organization was founded."**
>
> Donald T. Phillips, *Lincoln on Leadership*

Communicate Results to Improve Public Image

- Report facts showing results and value of work
- Portray outcomes visually
- Use consistent branding with logo and mission
- Apologize for mistakes and plan for recovery from errors
- Tie victim outcomes to program and system outcomes, activities, and events
- Use letterhead to convey outcomes
- Incorporate outcomes and successes in all brochures and public materials

and service usage by the public. A common logo, mission, goal, and public image also tie different agency programs and services together. However, don't expect a single message to encompass all victims, their needs, and their successes.

The same truth applies to direct victim services. There are commonalities in direct services, and yet victims may not fit into preconceived notions of victim outcomes. A balance is critical between understanding the likely core needs of victims, and listening for each victim's unique situation.

The advantage of knowing common victim outcomes is that several themes can capture in a few words the mission of the program. The ability to brand your program with a descriptive phrase, logo, and concept provides a distinctive and positive message, which, combined with demonstrable impact of services, will promote public confidence. Consistent marketing of outcomes and their measures provides the basis for an image and identity for the advocacy services. Choosing the right few words, concepts, and visual representations of the program's core victim outcomes is important in communicating to the public that supportive, effective services are ready and available.

Customer service is just as important in victim advocacy as it is in any other business. For example, staff should use the business practice of quickly and sincerely apologizing when an error is discovered or some victim service does not go well. Saying you are sorry means you are paying attention to their feelings and caring about errors that need to be corrected to improve their service.

In the case of victim advocacy, saying you are sorry is not necessarily an admittance of something done wrong, but rather something gone wrong from the victims perspective. Saying you are sorry conveys a listening, caring response by the service provider, and is an invitation for the victim to explain or complain further about the problem. A victim-centered service culture covets and values customer feedback. Victims should not fit into our services; our services should fit victim needs.

External uses of outcomes for guiding education and prevention efforts

Preventing crime is the best victim service. As noted earlier, preventive health will never eliminate the need for emergency rooms, and crime prevention will never eliminate the need to provide quality victim advocacy.

Preventing crime has many components. Much has been written on the goal of "hardening the target" of home, business, and neighborhood so criminals will go elsewhere. Additionally, common advice to the public is to not act like a victim. People are told to integrate behaviors of confidence, interpersonal distance, and listen to gut instincts of distrust. Security devices and other strategies supposedly will make anyone who employs them a difficult target (National Rifle Association, 1994).

Like a farmer's strategies to increase crop yield without control over the amount and timing of critical rains, these strategies may or may not have an overall statistical impact. In short, perpetrators often select convenient and vulnerable victims: children, subordinates, the mentally or physically incapacitated, the developmentally disabled, family members, neighbors, the drug- and alcohol-dependent, the socially atypical or isolated, and people with trusting or compliant personality types.

Having a victim outcome logic model allows you to use common victim needs to encourage victims to escape and report crime. Whether they suffer school bullying, acquaintance sexual assault, or elder abuse, current and potential victims can identify with others experiencing the same specific type of crime. Focusing public attention on specific victim needs for crime-specific safety, healing, justice, and financial problems encourages victims to believe their experiences and traumas are common, believable, and worth their effort to reach out for help. Hearing previous victims' reflections of their needs, current victims may be willing to step forward for victim advocacy help.

Public education is more effective when describing the personal stories and needs of victims, rather than just program descriptions. For example, a photo and caption are more powerful images than a commentary, and a story is often more persuasive than simple facts. Victims overcoming trauma and then transforming their experiences from victim into survivor, thriver, and successful coach for other victims' recovery is our outcome heaven. People can learn from others' experiences.

In some crimes, intervention by victim services can stop or reduce future crimes. Stalking, domestic violence, family sexual assault, and other crimes are often ongoing crimes that law enforcement and victim advocacy can deter by getting involved. However, victims are in the drivers' seats for making their own choices in life. Victim service professionals must not presume a *right choice,* and courts should not impose requirements on victims (a few legal exceptions allow court ordered mandates, such as in cases involving child abuse). Nevertheless, crime prevention is an important allied field and Victim Advocates must address revictimization prevention.

Expert advocacy skills can detect attitudes and behaviors in victims that will be useful in assuring safety and recovery. For example, using the common desire for a stable life and personal safety, Victim Advocates can promote positive choices and safety options. Peer counseling, support

Education and Prevention Ideas

- Integrate age and victimization-specific messages
  - Name the issues for school bullying, sexual assault, or elder abuse
- Promote victim rights and services regarding outcomes
  - Justice is not served until victims are
  - The U.S. Constitution needs to prescribe that victims should be informed, present, heard, repaid, and safe
- Link prevention to outcome harm in messages to public
  - "Your income and bank account are private. Report scams!"
  - "Your home should be safe. Report stalkers!"

Crime Prevention and Revictimization

- Redefine crime prevention to include prevention of revictimization

  - Expand efforts from marking property and "hardening the target" to preventing revictimization

- Redefine prevention to include long-term outcomes

  - Prevent suicides, generational cycles of violence, and systemic/cultural oppression

groups, and victim-to-victim impact panels may be eye-opening opportunities for victims seeking alternatives.

Preventing revictimization involves more than just preventing new crimes. It includes the overall mental health of victims, interrupting generational cycles of violence, and helping victims out of blatantly unhealthy situations. Substance abuse, addictions, suicides, and personal and familial dysfunction are issues that must be recognized and addressed in long-term victim outcomes. Freedom from crime includes freedom from the effects of crime.

Knowing the four primary injuries (and subsequent needs) of victims—physical (safety), psychological and spiritual (healing), injustice (fairness, respect, and legal rights), and financial (reimbursement and stability)—allows prevention efforts to identify the personal violation triggers important to the public. Certainly, for some people fear of a criminal violation is not real until it happens to them. Focusing on the trauma and injustice experienced by crime victims, and the available opportunities for hope and healing services, helps the public understand and reach out to victims and *do justly*.

Chapter 7 Summary: Applying Outcomes Externally

Your outcomes define you to your victims and to the public.

1. Your outcomes are your language and story to help keep a laser focus with partners and donors on the reason your program exists.

2. Once you have found some common and initial outcomes for the victims you serve, you can invite them to help you market your availability and expertise to unreached victims.

3. Your outcomes are key to attracting funding. Clear outcome logic models and measurement processes identify for grantors that you have an integrated plan that includes partners, incremental indicators of success, and long-term strategies. Focused, realistic, and visionary goals entice funders who are looking to invest in making discernible differences in people's lives.

4. Well defined outcomes result in a clear public image. They tell your story to victims and the public that you work hard, efficiently, purposely, expertly, and that your work results in changed lives. Outcomes are not the box you fit victims into; rather, they are the open-ended services that fit victim needs. Your outcomes are your brand; what people think of when they see your logo, mission statement, letterhead, public service announcements, newsletters, etc.

5. Outcomes are the basis for educating staff, partners, and future professionals in the art of victim advocacy and recovery. The ability to summarize the trauma, needs, and hopes of prior victims is a link to promoting positive choices, safety options, and interventions to prevent victimization. Mature long-term outcomes include the generational, systemic, substance abuse, Post-Traumatic Stress Disorder, suicidal, and related effects of violence and crime.

Chapter 8

Connecting the Dots

The sun is there even if you can't see it right now

How do you know if you are on the right track?

If you, your staff, your partners, and the program leadership more clearly understand what differences your program is trying to make in peoples' lives (why the program exists), and how to accomplish and more precisely measure that change (linking work to success), then you are on the right track. The greatest benefit to quality and outcome measures and logic models is the *process* of thinking through and believing in your work. Victim service leaders desire *efficient effort for effective change* in victims' lives. The goal is doing the right thing for each victim with passion. That is our calling: passionate and precise advocacy. We want to be immersed in meeting victim-driven needs, not skimming along offering passive mass assistance. Our primary desire in evaluation is to improve victims' lives, not produce research to prove theories and practices (W.K. Kellogg Foundation Evaluation Handbook, 2004).

An outcome model helps harmonize the seemingly random victim experiences with justice procedures, emotional pain, financial recovery, and safety fears. Outcomes bring focus and connect the dots between services, rights, eliminating violence against women, and addressing the broken relationships from crime. Outcomes help create the map of the victim assistance universe. They help us understand what we need to know and what to do to maneuver victims through the justice system and recovery process. The map can guide research and training standards for Victim Advocates.

Outcomes can guide victims in their self-help process. A map for Victim Advocates is by definition a map for their customers. An outcome focus dovetails with the need for self-help guides for victims, so our consumers will be able to guide us better while increasing control over their own lives.

You can use Kellogg Foundation templates to start understanding, planning, and designing existing or future victim services and programs. [See Exhibits 3-3d] Choose the template that you need for a new service you want to implement, a theoretical design, or to outline a current

> *Victim service leaders desire efficient effort for effective change in victims' lives. The goal is doing the right thing for each victim with passion.*

program. The point is to learn what improvements in victim's lives you are aiming for, and deliberately link your resources, activities, outputs, expenses, and partners to reach those outcomes in an incremental and measureable progression.

As you implement quality and outcome measures, there are assessment steps to guide your progress. Answer the following questions periodically to confirm your progress to-date with the anecdotal, survey, or research evidence you have available:

1. Can victims access services better? Has an assessment been completed? Have changes been implemented to increase outreach? Have you documented improvements in victims finding and reaching services?

2. Are services meeting victim needs? Have possible disconnects between victim needs and services been examined? Have any weaknesses been found? Have any changes in assessing, monitoring, or providing services resulted?

3. Are victims being treated more respectfully and uniquely? Has leadership used the audit tool with victims and staff to assess customer service? Have gaps in cultural and language communication, understanding of services, and respectful treatment been identified? Have staff procedures, training, or attitudes been changed to improve victim comfort levels and tailored services?

4. Are the safety, healing, justice, and financial stability outcomes correct for the population being served? Does the outcome model reflect the early needs (initial outcomes) of victims and the ultimate mission (long-term outcomes) of the organization?

5. Are the outcomes linked? In the outcome model, does each initial outcome logically and realistically link (horizontally) to other early victim needs? Are they linked with specific inputs, activities, and outputs? Are they linked (vertically) to future more complex outcomes?

6. Are the outcomes specific? Do activities flow to indicators? Do indicators flow to measurable outcome levels?

7. Are the outcomes being measured? Is the indicator source, collection method, and final measure a true reflection of the outcome (recognizing influencing factors, statistical deviations, indicator imperfections, etc.)?

Do not stop here. If you find the data dizzying, the facts fuzzy, and answers anguishing, remember the realistic goal is progress, not perfection. Take heart, attaining the right direction and organizational culture

If you find the data dizzying, the facts fuzzy, and answers anguishing, remember the realistic goal is progress, not perfection.

is both the most important and difficult accomplishment in the never-ending campaign for quality. Every Victim Advocate, administrator, and support staff member who "gets it" can make a difference. Step forward by prioritizing areas for focus, and then sharpen your specific assessments, monitoring tools, and outcome model designs. If progress is reasonable, even with imperfect measures and results, the quality and outcome plan for the program will serve to guide the way. A systemized process to plan, manage, and evaluate services will help focus and inspire further progress (Lewis, 2000).

Every Victim Advocate, administrator, and support staff member who "gets it" can make a difference.

The next sets of instructions are a guide for your imagination and tasks in making progress in quality and outcome progress.

1. Summarize the learning to-date with staff and advisors (e.g. supervisors, board of directors, victim service directors), and create a plan to integrate that learning to improve access, structure, process and outcomes. Take time for congratulations, celebrations, and communication of progress.

2. Estimate the budget implications and implementation barriers that result from the improvement plan.

3. Prioritize actionable areas of the plan and revise the plan design specific to tasks, staff assignments, and timelines. Then document it and start it.

4. Use intuition and assessment tools to asses the degree to which staff understand and integrate quality and outcomes in advocacy with each victim and in their definition of success (Brown and Sturdevant Reed, 2002).

If you can develop staff to have a high degree of intentional and continual quality and positive outcomes, you could be a millionaire. That vexing problem of continuous improvement with a laser focus on integrating quality into the entire workforce and workplace is the challenge for every organized human endeavor (Dennis, 2006). If every person of faith, corporation and manufacturing employee, and retail store associate were equally knowledgeable and committed to the vision and mission of their religion or organization, we would have created nearly perfect systems out of an imperfect world.

That vexing problem of continuous improvement with a laser focus on integrating quality into the entire workforce and workplace is the challenge for every organized human endeavor.

There is one more question which emphasizes another hill to climb in victim advocacy: Have we learned how to reduce revictimization? Even if and when we have, we may find that any improvements in revictimization rates are matched with increased predatory and violent offenders. In any case, we must act. By carefully listening to victims, and carefully adapting victims services to be linked with outcomes, we can begin to reduce revictimization. With informed action and hope, reducing revictimization may not be as difficult as we fear.

The notion that our best is good enough is also a problem. Our best is only good enough for today. Tomorrow we can, and must, improve. Outcome and quality measures demonstrate in theory and practice that experienced and excellent Victim Advocates can improve if they want to and if they have the right guidance.

Our best is only good enough for today. Tomorrow we can, and must, improve.

How do you manage a victim-outcome based program?

The hike toward a culture focused on outcomes is along the shifting path of organizational quality measures of access, structure, and process, and a fine-tuned strategic planning, management, and evaluation process. The goal of reaching the view at the peak of the mountain should not blind us to the beautiful scenery along the way—that is, our outcome successes every day. Daily success is when:

1. Victim outcomes are illuminated—goals and cultures clarified
2. Programs are aligned with outcomes—structures and alignments clarified
3. Services are linked to programs and outcomes—processes and inter-connections clarified
4. Influencing factors are analyzed and addressed—significance and role issues clarified
5. Indicators of success are established—scores and standards clarified
6. Services are provided—application and usefulness clarified
7. Results are evaluated—paths and boundaries clarified
8. Improvements are implemented—plan and focus clarified
9. Outcomes are achieved—models and goals verified
10. Lives are changed—our purpose and our passion verified

It is not magic that changes a victim's life. Some of the key ingredients of change include:

1. Adequate inputs of funding and information
2. Victim-centered organizational qualities of access, structure, and process
3. The ability of staff and leadership to look beyond the daily tasks
4. Advocates listening for and learning about each victim's unique needs
5. Society and stakeholders believing that doing right by victims matters
6. Improving services with consistent monitoring, analyzing, and data reintegration
7. Wise innovations and adaptations of victim advocacy
8. Passion for individual victim recovery

How can strong management produce successful results?

National victim outcomes consultant, J. Douglas Bailey, summarizes the strategic planning and management process in the following two graphics and explanation (J. Douglas Bailey, personal communication, January 31, 2008):

The top arc of the cycle is "planning." The bottom half is "implementation." Strategic program management requires us to take the long view

Managing for Results

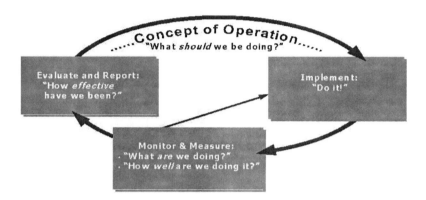

of both halves of the cycle, not just the box that reads, "Do it!" Administrators must escape the daily dictatorship of "Do it!" They must see past the impossible workloads (efforts) and unrelenting demands for service quality (compliance and satisfaction), seeking out the challenges facing our communities, the needs of our target populations and the results of our program design assumptions.

Planning: Management decisions focused on "What should we be doing?" This includes clarifying the community problems, victim needs, service responses to victim needs, and prioritizing among scarce resources. It defines our "Concept of Operation."

Implementation: Service delivery described as "This is what we DO—provide services"

Monitor and Measure: Part of implementation that is not direct services. It is the CHECK stage for answering: 1. "What **are** we doing?" and then feeding back into the implementation stage to "get it right" (represented in the graphic above with a small arrow angling to the Implementation box); 2. "How **well** are we doing it?" When we learn that we are doing what we said we would do, but we are doing it without quality, then we can also take immediate action to improve the process of service delivery.

Evaluate and Report: Asks the question, "How **effective** have we been?" This question is about tracking our client outcomes—our program's purpose, not about how well we perform against our own standards. This information adds to the evidence on effectiveness so we can adjust our program designs. What works becomes a new service model or best practice. What doesn't work can be changed to adopt those practices that do work.

Measurement is not a substitute for evaluation, but it can be a great supplement. Outcome measurement asks, "What happened to the victim?" not, "To which services may we attribute the changes in the victim?" Measurement is a management tool for identifying opportunities for program improvement, and not "proof" of impact or cost-effectiveness. Outcome measurement—usually the ongoing collection of victim self-reported changes and observable behaviors—is useful for management decision making. However, it is not capable of determining causality (i.e. "this service caused this outcome") because outcome measurement does not attempt to control intervening variables (Bailey, 2004).

Below is a slightly more detailed version of a strategic management model from J. Douglas Bailey:

> *Measurement is not a substitute for evaluation, but it can be a great supplement. Outcome measurement asks, "What happened to the victim?" not, "To which services may we attribute the changes in the victim?" J. Douglas Bailey*

Detailed Strategic Management Model

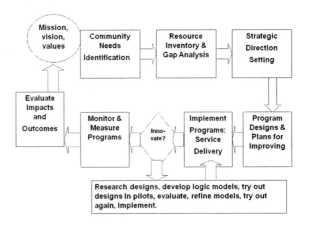

Concluding Thoughts for this Guide

Doing quality work and measuring its results are not fads. Victims' needs are real and victimization rates are high, with one in three adults and almost 70% of adolescents becoming victims of crime in their lifetimes (Menard, 2002). Funding sources and victims will never stop asking if we know what we are doing, and if we are really making a difference. The concept of outcomes will evolve but not vaporize. There is no sunset for quality.

A worldview that integrates individual services with systems change is required to stop victimization (Underwood and Edmunds, 2003). The U.S. Department of Justice has published a compendium of changes needed in, "New Directions from the Field: Victims' Rights and Services for the 21st Century" (U.S. Department of Justice, 1998). The conclusion of the "Decade for Change Report" regarding domestic violence states that there are four key themes: public awareness, education and training, outreach to and inclusion of men, and outreach to youth. It also states, "Only with a multi-layered, multi-level approach will these approaches succeed in changing social norms and public attitudes that will save lives and families of millions" (National Domestic Violence Hotline, 2007).

Victim driven outcomes are the best markers of success. However, even when we have a researched outcome logic model with services linked to each outcome, a quality program cannot ignore the problems of victims finding the services, benefiting from the right services, and being treated kindly and uniquely while receiving services. Organizational quality issues are intimately linked to achieving the safety, healing, justice, and financial recovery outcomes of victims. Good outcome models and organizational qualities must be integrated into the daily fabric of program processes and staff functions if victim driven outcomes are to be the DNA of victim services. Victim services are part of a moving river, and programs that simply tread water and maintain services are losing ground. Achieving victim needs can only happen if victim service design and culture—with collaboration (or at least neutrality) from the justice system and society—are centered on victim outcomes.

Victim services are part of a moving river, and programs that simply tread water and maintain services are losing ground.

This is a holy and human journey. People are not perfect, don't know it all, can't remember it all, and need help refocusing occasionally. We need guideposts like quality and outcomes goals. We continue to discover what service functions, skills, and relationships among Victim Advocates, victims, justice professionals, clergy, and family members are linked with improved victims' lives. Our notion of an improved life may feel negligible compared to a victim's injury or loss of a loved one. A sense of not being alone may be the only improvement in their early stages of despair.

Readers may know some routes and short cuts absent from this guide, but which worked for their unique situations. No two people provide care in the same way and no two victims have exactly the same needs. Nevertheless, humans have a lot in common, and with shared experiences and research, identifiable points on the map of victim recovery are appearing.

Even as a "Model T" version of victim advocacy, this guide should reflect basic future concepts similar to ones developed for other populations

(The Council on Quality and Leadership, 2005). It is more like a hand drawn experience-based map rather than a research-based or precise Global Positioning System system. Since many of the concepts in this guide are experience-based, there are limits to their reliability and validity. Some themes were merged, outcomes reworded, and concepts defined so as to simplify the models and language. The goal was accuracy, yet without letting "the perfect be the enemy of the good."

The hopes and the horrors of life reflect many juxtapositions and paradoxes, including the fact that humans are both unique and common. Wisdom involves believing that each person we serve is our brother or sister with a fragile and permanent soul equal to our own. Even if that is not your exact religious language or faith, we must believe that life is precious and that we can make a difference in people's lives every day.

Chapter 8 Summary: Connecting the Dots

Quality measures and logic models are particularly valuable for refocusing Victim Advocates on victims' needs and program methodology to achieve those needs. Informed passion results in efficient effort for effective change. Achieving accurate indicators and measures of success must be both practiced-based and research-informed, as research is not the primary task of service providers. Quality services are possible by ensuring that victims can find you, their needs are being met, they are treated with respect, and their needs for safety, healing, justice, and financial recovery are met. Achieving quality requires leadership, vision, vigilant monitoring, and coaching. This map toward successful victim advocacy is, by definition, also a map for individual victims seeking self-help guidance. This endeavor can be enjoyable and rewarding as victim needs continue to be met and staff continue to work in synchronization. There are limits to many of the suggestions in this guide as they are not researched-based. However, there is no doubt that quality victim services can result in minimizing victims' horror and maximizing their hope.

Selected Outcome & Logic Model Resources

1. University of Wisconsin web site. Go to www.uwex.edu/ces/lmcourse and click "Connect to course content." It is free and includes work by Ellen Taylor-Powell, Ph.D., and sample logic models, teaching tools, and outcome summaries.

2. Texas Association Against Sexual Assault (www.taasa.org—go to "resources" then "TAASA Publications" then "Other Publications" and click on "Outcome Measures for Sexual Assault Services in Texas" (93 pages, August, 2003). The site also has Sexual Assault Outcome Measures - Tools (30 pages). Includes Outcome Models for services: Accompaniment; Crisis Intervention Services; Education Services; Follow-up Services; Hotline Services; Peer & Therapeutic Counseling; Volunteer Program, and Data Collection Forms for each. Free

3. Outcome evaluation strategies for sexual assault service program: A practical guide, (107 pages) by Cris M. Sullivan, Ph.D., and S. Coats, MSW, (2000). Contact Michigan Coalition Against Domestic and Sexual Violence (MCADSV), at telephone # 1-517-347-7000 or send check to: MCADSV, 3893 Okemos Rd., Suite B3, Okemos, Michigan, 48864. $40 (includes shipping and handling)

4. Outcome evaluation strategies for domestic violence programs: A practical guide, (102 pages) by Cris M. Sullivan, Ph.D., (1998). Contact Pennsylvania Coalition Against Domestic Violence (PCADV), at telephone # 1-800-932-4632 or send check to: PCADV, 6400 Flank Dr., Suite 1300, Harrisburg, Pennsylvania, 17112. $25 (for non-profits, cost includes shipping and handling)

5. Measuring Program Outcomes: A Practical Approach,(169 pages), United Way of America (1996). Go to web site: http://www.unitedwaystore.com and search with "outcomes". One of the best "walk through" manuals for learning outcomes. $5 (plus $6 for shipping & handling)

6. United Way of America web site: http://national.unitedway.org. Search using "outcome resources." Has numerous reports and studies on outcomes used by non-profits around the nation. Free

7. Standards for Victim Assistance Programs and Providers, from the National Victim Assistance Standards Consortium, May 2003, 141 pages. Go to Web site: http://www.sc.edu and search "victim standards." Includes chapters on the consortium, standards, terminology, definition & mission statement, values, program standards, competency standards, ethical standards, implementing standards, sample assessment tools, promising practices, directory of credentialing programs and related standards, resources, and more. Free

8. Performance Measurement: Getting Results, Second Edition, by Harry P. Hatry (soft cover), 2006 (342 pages), published by The Urban Institute Press, Publisher ID# 211405. 2100 M Street, N.W., Washington, D.C., 20037. ISBN # 0-87766-7349. Order at web site: www.uipress.org. A comprehensive and readable guide on developing and using outcomes. $34.50

9. Performance Vistas, Inc. website: www.performancevistas.org. Tel: (770) 992-0679. It is a non-profit consulting firm whose mission is to help agencies improve their service provision and management systems and promote organizational learning. Offers DVD $15.95 (plus $3.50 shipping and handling), computer-assisted instruction guide $44.95 (plus $5.00 shipping & handling), and many free downloads.

10. W.K. Kellogg Foundation Logic Model Development Guide provides practical assistance to nonprofits engaged in planning and evaluation. See four samples in this guide at Exhibit 3 (3, 3a, 3b, 3c, and 3d). For more information, got to http://www.wkkf.org and search "logic models."

Top Ten Glossary

1. Access—Program quality area measuring the degree that services are visible, reachable, acceptable, and available to each victim at their time of need.

2. Activities—Part of a logic model; the work you do/the services you provide. Activities include the strategies, techniques, and types of treatment that comprise the program's methodology (United Way of America, 1996).

3. Inputs—Part of a logic model; the resources and constraints that permit an organization to function (e.g. money, staff, facilities, laws, policies, equipment)

4. Indicator—A marker of the degree to which progress and success is attained; like a point on a map informs you of your progress toward your destination. An observable and measurable item conveys evidence of progress toward a goal.

5. Logic Model—A design or graphic that reflects the content, sequence, and purpose of your program. It shows how all the parts and strategies of your program are linked together.

6. Outcome—Part of a logic model; program quality area measuring the degree that: 1. A persons' life is affected (a victim outcome) in his/her safety, healing, justice, or financial recovery, or; 2. The access, structure, or process of a program is impacted (a program outcome) as service or organizational goals are met.

7. Output—Part of a logic model; the type and amount of victims helped and work produced. Described numerically, such as the number of people served or hours of service delivered.

8. Process—Program quality area measuring how victims are treated in areas of ethics, professionalism, uniqueness, and sensitivity.

9. Structure—Program quality area measuring the organizational framework of governance, partnerships, tools, staff, and correct services for each victim.

10. Victim Advocacy—Victim-centered profession and culture that prioritizes meeting victim-driven needs, both individual and systemic.

Acierno, R. & Kilpatrick, D. (2003). Mental health needs of crime victims: epidemiology & outcomes. *Victimization Journal of Traumatic Stress, 16 (2)*, 124-125.

Adams, D. Personal Communication, December 15, 2009. Lima, Ohio.

Authenticity Consulting LLC. *Nonprofit Organizational Assessment.* Retrieved on September 9, 2009 from http://www.surveymonkey.com/s.asp?u=3754722401

Bailey, J.D. (2004). *Managing for Results: Participants Workbook*, and *Facilitators Process Guidebook. A Logical Approach for Program Design, Outcome Measurement and Process Evaluation.* Atlanta, Performance Vistas, Inc.

Barker, K., Burdick, D., Stek, J., Wessel, W., & Youngblood, R. (1995). *The NIV Study Bible.* Grand Rapids, MI: Zondervan Publishing House.

Barry, B. W. (1997). *Strategic Planning Workbook for Nonprofit Organizations.* Saint Paul, MN: Amherst H. Wilder Foundation.

Boland, M.L. (1997). *Crime Victim's Guide to Justice.* Naperville, IL: Sourcebooks, Inc.

Brickman, E. (2002). *Development of a national study of victim needs and assistance.* [electronic version] Retrieved on September 9, 2009 from http://www.ncjrs.gov/pdffiles1/nij/grants/195625.pdf

Brown, R.E., Sturdevant Reed, C. *An Integral Approach to Evaluating Outcome Evaluation Training*, American Journal of Evaluation. 2002;23;1. Retrieved on September 9, 2009 from http://aje.sagepub.com/cgi/reprint/23/1/1

Buddhas Village. (2004). *Compassion: A Religion for All.* Retrieved September 9, 2009 from http://www.buddhasvillage.com/teachings/hh_compassion.htm

Burt, M., Harrell, A., Newmark, L., Aron, L., Jacobs, L. (1997). *Evaluation Guidebook for Projects Funded by S.T.O.P. Formula Grants Under the Violence Against Women Act.* Retrieved on September 9, 2009 from http://www.ojp.usdoj.gov/BJA/evaluation/guide/documents/stop1-4.html

Campbell, R. (2006). Rape Survivors' Experiences with the Legal and

Medical Systems: Do Rape Victim Advocates Make a Difference? *Violence Against Women,* 12 (1), 30-44.

Consolidated Victim Service Program Standards. (2009). *Pennsylvania Commission on Crime and Delinquency.* Retrieved on September 9, 2009 from http://www.portal.state.pa.us/portal/server.pt?open =512&objID=5418&&SortOrder=2&level=3&parentid=5416& css=L3&mode=2

Carden, F., Earl, S., & Smutylo, T. (2001). *Outcome Mapping: Building Learning and Reflection into Development Programs.* Ottawa, Ontario, Canada: International Research Development Centre.

CDC—RPE Logic Model. (2007). *Creating Safer Communities: Rape Prevention Education Model of Community Change Final Draft— January 31, 2007.* Retrieved on September 9, 2009 from http:// www.oag.state.tx.us/victims/grants/sapcs/guidance/Appendix%20 D1.1.pdf

Checklist for Accountability. (2005). Retrieved on September 9, 2009 from http://www.independentsector.org/issues/accountability/checklist/ index.html

Coldren, Jr., J.R., Bynum, T., & Thome, J. (2001, 2nd printing). *OJJDP, Evaluating Juvenile Justice Programs: A Design Monograph for State Planners.* Retrieved on September 9, 2009, from http://www.ojp. usdoj.gov/BJA/evaluation/guide/documents/documentg.html

Cowan, J., Hatry, H. P., & Hendricks, M. (2004). *Analyzing Outcome Information: Getting the Most from Data.* Retrieved on September 9, 2009 from http://www.urban.org/UploadedPDF/310973_ OutcomeInformation.pdf

Curran, M. (2008). *WSCADV, Moving from Rules to Rights and Responsibilities.* Retrieved on September 9, 2009 from http://www. wscadv.org/resourcesAlpha.cfm?aId=D00CC786-C298-58F6- 0B41D2ABA36C4E39

Dennis, P. (2006). *Getting the Right Things Done.* Cambridge, MA: The Lean Enterprise Institute.

Derene, S., Bailey, J.D., Montagnino, S. (2004). *Recommendations to the Office for Victims of Crime (OVC) on Revisions to VOCA Victim Assistance Data Collection.* Conference of National Association of VOCA Assistance Administrators [NAVAA].

Detailed Information on the Crime Victim's Programs Assessment. (2006). Retrieved on September 13, 2008 from http://www.whitehouse. gov/OMB/expectmore/detail/10003815.2006.html

Donabedian, A. (1998). *Performance Indicators for Rehabilitation Programs, version 1.1.* Retrieved on September 9, 2009 from www.carf.org/ pdf/PerIndMo.pdf

Edleson, J. L. (1997). *Evaluating Domestic Violence Programs.* Minneapolis, MN: Domestic Abuse Project.

"Focusing Police Efforts on Repeat Victims Advocated: Helps Those Most In Need and Is a Major Means of Reducing Crime." (1997, March/April). *The Crime Victims Report,* 8.

Foster, P., Reinelt, C., Sullivan, S. (2002). *Evaluating Outcomes and Impacts: A Scan of 55 Leadership Development Programs.* Retrieved on September 9, 2009 from http://www.wkkf.org/Pubs/CCT/ Leadership/Pub3780.pdf

Francis, K. (2000). *Gauging Progress: A Guidebook for Community Sexual Assault Programs and Community Development Initiatives.* Retrieved on September 9, 2009 from http://new.vawnet.org/Assoc_Files_ VAWnet/GaugingProgress.pdf

Frederick, L., Lizdas, K.C. (2003). *The Role of Restorative Justice in the Battered Women's Movement.* Retrieved on September 9, 2009 from http://data.ipharos.com/bwjp/documents/restroative_justice.pdf

Gabbay, Z. D. (2005). *Justifying Restorative Justice: A Theoretical Justification for the Use of Restorative Justice Practices.* Retrieved on September 9, 2009 from http://www.realjustice.org/library/justifyingrj.html

Hatry, H., Houten, T., Plantz, M.C., & Taylor Greenway, M. (1996). *Measuring Program Outcomes: A Practical Approach.* Alexandria, LA: United Way of America.

Hendricks, M. Personal Communication, April 3-5, 2007. Lima, Ohio.

Illingworth, R., (2002, August). *Arizona's VOCA Outcome Measures.* Annual conference of National Association of VOCA Assistance Administrators, Atlanta, GA.

Innovation Network. (2005). *Point K Learning Center free tools and resources for nonprofits.* Retrieved on September 9, 2009 from http://www.

innonet.org/index.php?section_id=64&content_id=185

Internal Revenue Service. *Governance and Related Topics 501(c)(3) Organizations.* Retrieved on September 9, 2009 from http://www.irs.gov/pub/irs-tege/governance_practices.pdf

Jenkins, B. (1999). *What to do When the Police Leave: A Guide to the First Days of Traumatic Loss* (2nd ed.). Arlington, VA: Washington Business Journal Press.

Jewish Publication Society Tanakh. (1917). Micah Chapter 6 verse 8.

Kass-Bartelmes, B.L., & Rutherford, M.K. (2004). *Women and domestic violence: programs and tools that improve care for victims.* Retrieved on September 9, 2009 from http://www.ahrq.gov/RESEARCH/domviolria/domviolria.pdf

Kilpatrick, D. (2003). Editor's Note. *Journal of Traumatic Stress*, 16 (2), 115.

Lamm Weisel, D. (2005). *Analyzing Repeat Victimization.* Retrieved on September 9, 2009 from http://www.cops.usdoj.gov/files/ric/Publications/e07055803.pdf

Lampkin, L.M. & Morley, E. (2004). *Using Outcome Information: Making Data Pay Off.* Retrieved on September 9, 2009 from http://www.urban.org/UploadedPDF/311040_OutcomeInformation.pdf

Lewis, A. (2000). Nonprofit Organizational Assessment Tool Outcome Measurement. Retrieved on September 9, 2009 from http://www.uwex.edu/ces/cced/nonprofits/management/assessment.cfm

List-Warrilow, J., & Menard, A. (2007, September). Improving advocacy. *Synergy, the Newsletter of the Resource Center on Domestic Violence: Child Protection and Custody,* 2-5.

Lowenstein, T.K. (2000, August). Against Execution. *The American Prospect,* 2.

Lord, J.H. (2006). *How to Provide Spiritually Sensitive Trauma Care.* Retrieved on September 9, 2009 from http://www.giftfromwithin.org/html/provide.html

Manis Findley, K. (2004). *If this is Not a Place: A Violence Prevention and Intervention Training Curriculum for Communities of Faith and*

Clergy. Little Rock, AR: The Center for Healing and Hope.

McNamara, C. (1997-2007). *Basic Guide to Outcomes-Based Evaluation for Nonprofit Organizations with Very Limited Resources.* Retrieved on September 9, 2009 from http://www.managementhelp.org/evaluatn/outcomes.htm

Menard, S. (2002). *OJJDP, Short- and long-term consequences of adolescent victimization.* Retrieved on September 9, 2009 from http://www.ncjrs.gov/pdffiles1/ojjdp/191210.pdf

Mental Health Response to Mass Violence and Terrorism: A Field Guide. (2005). Retrieved on September 9, 2009 from http://mentalhealth.samhsa.gov/publications/allpubs/SMA05-4025/

Messing, T.J. (2007-2008). Research & Practice in Cahoots: A Guide to Research for Practitioners. Zorza, J (Ed.). *Domestic Violence Report, 12-13, 2–1.*

Michigan Coalition Against Domestic Violence and Sexual Violence. (2004). *Reporting Sexual Assault: A Guide for Journalists.* Okemos, MI: PUBLISHER.

Michigan Coalition Against Domestic Violence and Sexual Violence. (2007). *Working with the Media: A Toolkit for Service Providers.* Okemos, MI: Author.

Michigan Crime Victim Services Commission. (2003). *Program Evaluation for VOCA Grantees: Level 2.* Okemos, MI: Michigan Public Health Institute.

Michigan Public Health Institute. (1998). *Introduction to Evaluation Training & Practice for Sexual Assault Service Delivery.* Data Systems, Evaluation and Training. Okemos, MI.

Morley, E., Vinson, E., & Hatry, H.P. (2001). *Outcome Measurement in Nonprofit organizations: Current Practices and Recommendations.* Retrieved on September 9, 2009 from http://www.independentsector.org/programs/research/outcomes.pdf

National Center on Outcomes Resources. (2001). *Practice Guidance for Delivering Outcomes in Service Coordination.* Retrieved on September 15, 2008, from http://thecouncil.dreamhost.com/pdfs/service-coord.pdf

National Domestic Violence Hotline. (2007). *Decade for Change Report*, pg. 37. Retrieved on September 9, 2009 from http://www.ndvh.org/decadeforchange/Decade%20for%20Change%20SUMMIT%20Report.pdf

National Rifle Association. (1994). *Women's Programs: Refuse to be a victim.* Retrieved on September 9, 2009 from http://www.nrahq.org/RTBAV

National Standards Manual. (n.d.) Retrieved on September 9, 2009 from http://www.sc.edu/ccfs/training/victimstandards.pdf

National Victim Bar Association. (n.d.) Retrieved on September 9, 2009 from www.victimbar.org

National Victims Constitutional Amendment Passage. (2003). Retrieved on September 9, 2009 from http://www.nvcap.org

Newmark, L.C. (2006). *Crime Victims Needs and VOCA-Funded Services: Findings and Recommendations from Two National Studies.* Retrieved on September 9, 2009 from http://www.ncjrs.gov/App/Publications/Abstract.aspx?ID=235795

Newmark, L.C. (August 21, 2001). *Victim Surveys: A Users' Primer With Examples from the National Evaluation of VOCA Programs.* Presented at National Organization for Victim Assistance 27th Annual Conference at Edmonton, Alberta, Canada.

Nnanabu, C. (2006). Crime Victims Compensation Program Logic Model. *Crime Victim Compensation Quarterly,* 2.

Nonprofit Organizational Effectiveness. (2006) Retrieved on September 9, 2009 from www.nonprofitcongress.org/?=capacitybuilding

Norman, R, Spencer, A., & Feder, G. (2007). Cost effectiveness analysis: what you always wanted to know but were afraid to ask. *Family Violence and Prevention Health Practice- An E-journal of the Family Violence Prevention Fund, Issue 5.*

Ochberg, F. (2003). Post Traumatic Stress Disorder. *National Center for Victims of Crime, Fall 2003/Winter 2003, 11-13.*

Panel on the Nonprofit Sector. (2005). *Strengthening transparency, governance, accountability of charitable organizations: A final report to Congress and Nonprofit Sector.* Retrieved October 6, 2008 from http://info.ethicspoint.com/files/PDF/resources/Panel_Final_Report.pdf

Patton, Michael, (2004). *Utilization Focused Evaluation.* Retrieved on September 14, 2008 from http://www.uic.edu/sph/mch/ce/mch_leadership2004/transcripts/keynote_transcript.htm

Pennsylvania Commission on Crime and Delinquency. (2003). *Use, Non-Use and Efficacy of Pennsylvania's Victim Service Programs, Final Report.* Retrieved on September 9, 2009 from http://www.pccd.state.pa.us/pccd/lib/pccd/stats/completedprojectdocs/vs_eval_final_report_3-18-04.pdf

Plantz, M.C., Taylor Greenway, M., Hendricks, M. (2008). *Outcome Measurement: Showing Results in the Nonprofit Sector.* Retrieved on September 9, 2009 from http://auth.unitedway.org/Outcomes/Library/ndpaper.cfm

Principles and Practices for Nonprofit Excellence: A guide to nonprofit board members, managers, and staff. (2005). Retrieved on September 9, 2009 from http://http.mncn.org/info/principles_and_practices.pdf

RAINN—Rape, Abuse & Incest National Network. (2008). *Effects of Sexual Assault.* Retrieved on September 9, 2009 from http://www.rainn.org/print/19

Romero, O. *The First Candle of the Justpeace Advent Wreath.* Retrieved on September 9, 2009 from http://www.justpeace.org/advent98-1.htm

Santa Barbara Rape Crisis Center. (2000). *Helping a Survivor.* Retrieved on September 9, 2009 from http://www.sbrapecrisiscenter.org/03Seeking%20Help/survivor2.html

Sims, B., Yost, B., & Abbott, C. (2006). The efficacy of victim services programs: alleviating the psychological suffering of crime victims. *Criminal Justice Policy Review,* 387-406.

Stark, E. (2000). Denver victim services 2000 needs assessment. *OVC Bulletin, October 2000, 9.*

Strategic Planning Toolkit. (2008). Retrieved on September 9, 2009 from https://www.ovcttac.gov/taresources/stratPlan.cfm

Sullivan, C., Alexy, C. (2001). *Evaluating the Outcomes of Domestic Violence Service Programs: Some Practical Considerations and Strategies.*

Retrieved on September 9, 2009, from http://new.vawnet.org/ Assoc_Files_VAWnet/AR_evaldv.pdf

Sullivan, C., Keefe, M. (1999). *Evaluations of Advocacy Efforts to End Intimate Male Violence Against Women.* Retrieved on September 9, 2009 from http://new.vawnet.org/category/Main_Doc. php?docid=382

Sullivan, C. M., Coats, S. (2003). *Outcome Evaluation Strategies for Sexual Assault Service Programs: A Practical Guide.* Okemos, MI: Michigan Coalition Against Domestic and Sexual Violence.

Taylor-Powell, E. (2005). *Logic Models: A framework for program planning and evaluation, University of Wisconsin-Extension-Cooperative Extension.* (2005). Retrieved on September 9, 2009 from http://www.uwex.edu/ces/pdande/Evaluation/powerpt/ nutritionconf05.ppt

Tewksbury, R., Moore, D. K., & King, N. N. (1998). Victims' Satisfaction with Prosecutors and Victim Advocates: A Case Study. In L. J. Moriarty & R A. Jerin (Eds.), *Current Issues In Victimology Research.* Durham, NC: Carolina Academic Press.

Texas Association Against Sexual Assault (2003). *Outcome Measures for Sexual Assault Services in Texas, Final Report.* Retrieved on September 9, 2009 from http://www.taasa.org/publications/ Outcome_Measures.pdf

The Council on Quality and Leadership. (2005). *Cross-walk between the CMS HCBS Quality Framework and CQL's Quality Measures.* Retrieved on September 14, 2008 from http://www.thecouncil. org/pdfs/cqlandcmscrosswalk05.pdf

The Forbes Funds. (2004). *Look Here. Attracting and Developing the NEXT GENERATION of Nonprofit Leaders.* Retrieved on September 9, 2000 from www.forbesfunds.org/docs/LookHere.pdf

The Principles Workbook: Steering Your Board Toward Good Governance and Ethical Practice. (2009). Retrieved on September 9, 2009 from http://www.nonprofitpanel.org/Report/principles/index. html#principles

Tjaden, P., Thoennes, N. (2006). *Extent, Nature, and Consequences of Rape Victimization: Findings from the National Violence Against Women Survey.* Retrieved on September 9, 2009 from http://www.ncjrs.

org/pdffiles1/nij/210346.pdf

Underwood, T.L. & Edmunds, C. (Eds.). (2003). *Victim Assistance: Exploring Individual Practice, Organizational Policy, and Societal Responses*. New York: Springer Publishing Company.

United Way of America. (1998). "United Way of America training material." Used with permission.

U.S. Department of Health and Human Services. (2005). *Mental Health Response to Mass Violence and Terrorism: A Field Guide*. Retrieved on September 9, 2009 from http://mentalhealth.samhsa.gov/publications/allpubs/SMA05-4025/SMA05-4025.pdf

U.S. Department of Justice. (1997). "Final Program Guidelines Victims of Crime Act FFY 1997." Washington, DC: The Federal Register.

U.S. Department of Justice. (1998). *New Directions from the Field: Victims' Rights and Services for the 21ˢᵗ Century.* Retrieved on September 9, 2009 from http://www.ojp.gov/ovc/newdirections/pdftxt/direct.pdf

U.S. Department of Justice. (2003). *Intimate Partner Homicide*, 250. Retrieved on September 9, 2009 from http://www.ncjrs.gov/pdffiles1/jr000250.pdf

U.S. Department of Justice. (2006). *2006 Biennial Report to Congress on the Effectiveness of Grant Programs Under the Violence Against Women Act.* Retrieved on September 9, 2009 from http://www.ovw.usdoj.gov/docs/ovw-measuring-effectiveness-report.pdf

U.S. Department of Justice. (n.d.) *Sexual Assault Advocate/Counselor Training.* Retrieved on September 9, 2009 from https://www.ovcttac.gov/saact/index.cfm

U.S. National Crime Victim's Rights Week. (2005). Retrieved on September 9, 2009 from http://www.ovc.gov/ncvrw/2005.html

Valley of the Sun United Way. (2008). *Logic Model Handbook.* Retrieved on September 9, 2009 from http://www.vsuw.org/file/logic_model_handbook_updated_2008.pdf

Victim Rights Law Center, Inc. (2008). *Beyond the Criminal Justice System: Using the Law to Help Restore the Lives of Sexual Assault Victims—A Practical Guide for Attorneys and Advocates.* Retrieved on September 9, 2009 from http://www.victimrights.org/pdf-manual/beyondthecriminaljusticesystem.pdf

Victims of Crime — A Social Work Response: Building Skills To Strengthen Survivors. (2006). Retrieved on September 9, 2009 from https://www.ovcttac.gov/taresources/socialwork.cfm

Victim Satisfaction with the Criminal Justice System. (2006). Retrieved on September 9, 2009 from http://www.ojp.usdoj.gov/nij/journals/253/victim.html

Walker, L.E. (2006). *Battered women syndrome: empirical findings.* Retrieved on October 6, 2008 from http://www3.interscience.wiley.com/journal/118570514/abstract?CRETRY=1&SRETRY=0

Welcome to Enhancing Program Performance with Logic Models. (2002). Retrieved on September 9, 2009 from http://www.uwex.edu/ces/lmcourse/interface/coop_M1_Overview.htm

Witmer, G., Emmerling, A., McManus, D. (2003, September). *Measuring Program Outcomes for Victim Services.* Workshop conducted at the Mid-Atlantic Sexual Assault Conference, Philadelphia, PA.

Witness Justice. (2008). *Sleep Tips for Trauma Victims.* Retrieved on September 9, 2009 from http://www.witnessjustice.org/resources/sleep.cfm

W.K. Kellogg Foundation Evaluation Handbook. (2004). Retrieved on September 9, 2009 from http://www.wkkf.org/Pubs/Tools/Evaluation/Pub770.pdf

W.K. Kellogg Foundation Logic Model Development Guide. (2004). Retrieved on September 9, 2009 from http://www.wkkf.org/Pubs/Tools/Evaluation/Pub3669.pdf

Young, M. A., Davis, R. C., Lurigio, A. J., Herman, S. (2007). "Introduction to Victims of Crime: The Interaction of Research and Practice." In C. Davis, A. J. Lurigio, & S. Herman (Eds.), *Victims of Crime* (3rd ed.). Thousand Oaks, CA: Sage Publications.

Yusuf, A. (1999). The Meaning of the Holy Qur'an. 10th Edition. Beltsville, MD: Amana Publications. Qur'an 2:231-233; 4:19-21; 16:90; 65:6.

Zehr, H., & Achilles, M. (1999). "Restorative Justice Signposts." Scottdale, PA: Mennonite Central Committee.

Zollinger, B.A., Wolfe, J., Ray, M., Walker, M. S., Paige, L. Z., Gross, L. (2007). *Domestic Violence Victim Services Awareness, Use, and Satisfaction Project.* Retrieved on September 7, 2008 from http://www.fhsu.edu/docking/img/Archives/Domestic%20 Violence%20Victim%20Services%20Final%20Report.pdf

Zweig, et al, (2003). *The effects on victims of victim service programs funded by the stop formula grants program.* Retrieved on September 9, 2009 from http://www.urban.org/publications/410645.htm

Zweig, J. M. & Burt, M.R. (2007). Predicting women's perceptions of domestic violence and sexual assault agency helpfulness: What matters to program clients. *Violence Against Women*, 13, 1149.

Exhibit 1

Exhibit 1 (Chapter 2)
Federal Performance-Based Measures
Quoted from U. S. Department of Justice

(www.ojp.gov/ovc/publications/infores/newdirections2000/global2.html)

Questions/Answers (Detailed Assessment)

Section 1 - Purpose and Design

1. Is the program purpose clear?
2. Does the program address a specific and existing problem, interest, or need?
3. Is the program designed so that it is not redundant or duplicative of any other Federal, state, local or private effort?
4. Is the program design free of major flaws that would limit the program's effectiveness or efficiency?
5. Is the program design effectively targeted so that resources will address the program's purpose directly and will reach intended beneficiaries?

Section 2 - Strategic Planning

1. Does the program have a limited number of specific long-term performance measures that focus on outcomes and meaningfully reflect the purpose of the program?
2. Does the program have ambitious targets and timeframes for its long-term measures?
3. Does the program have a limited number of specific annual performance measures that can demonstrate progress toward achieving the program's long-term goals?
4. Does the program have baselines and ambitious targets for its annual measures?
5. Do all partners (including grantees, sub-grantees, contractors, cost-sharing partners, and other government partners) commit to and work toward the annual and/or long-term goals of the program?
6. Are independent evaluations of sufficient scope and quality conducted on a regular basis or as needed to support program improvements and evaluate effectiveness and relevance to the problem, interest, or need?
7. Are budget requests explicitly tied to accomplishment of the annual and long-term performance goals, and are the resource needs presented in a complete and transparent manner in the program's budget?
8. Has the program taken meaningful steps to correct its strategic planning deficiencies?

Section 3 - Program Management

1. Does the agency regularly collect timely and credible performance information, including information from key program partners, and use it to manage the program and improve performance?
2. Are Federal managers and program partners (including grantees, sub-grantees, contractors, cost-sharing partners, and other government partners) held accountable for cost, schedule and performance results?
3. Are funds (Federal and partners') obligated in a timely manner, spent for the intended purpose and accurately reported?
4. Does the program have procedures (e.g. competitive sourcing/cost comparisons, IT improvements, appropriate incentives) to measure and achieve efficiencies and cost effectiveness in program execution?
5. Does the program collaborate and coordinate effectively with related programs?
6. Does the program use strong financial management practices?
7. Has the program taken meaningful steps to address its management deficiencies?
8. Does the program have oversight practices that provide sufficient knowledge of grantee activities?
9. Does the program collect grantee performance data on an annual basis and make it available to the public in a transparent and meaningful manner?

Section 4 - Program Results/Accountability

1. Has the program demonstrated adequate progress in achieving its long-term performance goals?
2. Does the program (including program partners) achieve its annual performance goals?
3. Does the program demonstrate improved efficiencies or cost effectiveness in achieving program goals each year?
4. Does the performance of this program compare favorably to other programs, including government, private, etc., with similar purpose and goals?
5. Do independent evaluations of sufficient scope and quality indicate that the program is effective and achieving results?

Exhibit 2a (Chapter 3)
Washington State Victim Compensation Program Logic Model

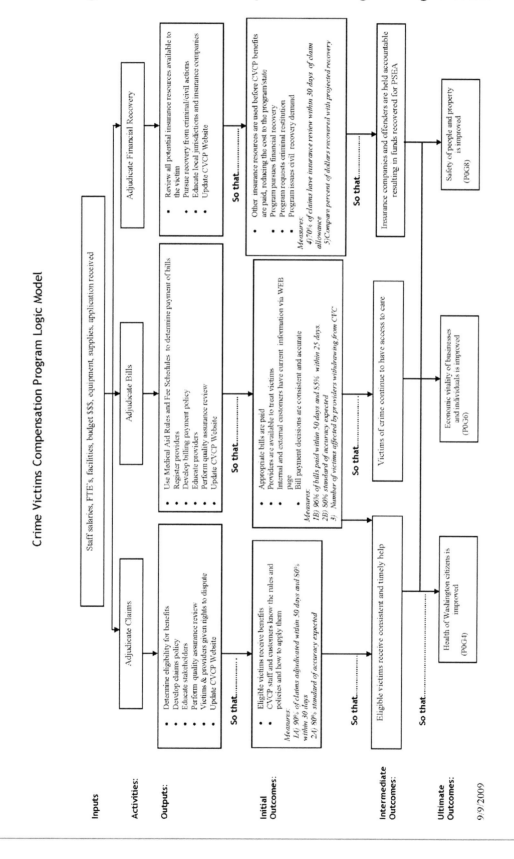

Crime Victims Compensation Program Logic Model

Inputs

Staff salaries, FTE's, facilities, budget $$$, equipment, supplies, application received

Activities:

Adjudicate Claims | Adjudicate Bills | Adjudicate Financial Recovery

Outputs:

Adjudicate Claims
- Determine eligibility for benefits
- Develop claims policy
- Educate stakeholders
- Perform quality assurance review
- Victims & providers given rights to dispute
- Update CVCP Website

Adjudicate Bills
- Use Medical Aid Rules and Fee Schedules to determine payment of bills
- Register providers
- Develop billing payment policy
- Educate providers
- Perform quality assurance review
- Update CVCP Website

Adjudicate Financial Recovery
- Review all potential insurance resources available to the victim
- Pursue recovery from criminal/civil actions
- Educate local jurisdictions and insurance companies
- Update CVCP Website

Initial Outcomes:

So that.....
- Eligible victims receive benefits
- CVCP staff and customers know the rules and policies and how to apply them

Measures:
1A) 90% of claims adjudicated within 50 days and 80% within 30 days
2A) 80% standard of accuracy expected

So that.....
- Appropriate bills are paid
- Providers are available to treat victims
- Internal and external customers have current information via WEB page
- Bill payment decisions are consistent and accurate

Measures:
1B) 96% of bills paid within 50 days and 55% within 25 days
2B) 80% standard of accuracy expected
3) Number of victims affected by providers withdrawing from CVC

So that.....
- Other insurance resources are used before CVCP benefits are paid, reducing the cost to the program/state
- Program pursues financial recovery
- Program requests criminal restitution
- Program issues civil recovery demand

Measures:
4) 70% of claims have insurance review within 30 days of claim allowance
5)Compare percent of dollars recovered with projected recovery

Intermediate Outcomes:

So that.....

Eligible victims receive consistent and timely help | Victims of crime continue to have access to care | Insurance companies and offenders are held accountable resulting in funds recovered for PSEA

Ultimate Outcomes:

So that.....

Health of Washington citizens is improved (P0G4) | Economic vitality of businesses and individuals is improved (P0G6) | Safety of people and property is improved (P0G8)

9/9/2009

Exhibit 2b (Chapter 3)
Center for Disease (CDC)—Rape Prevention Education Logic Model

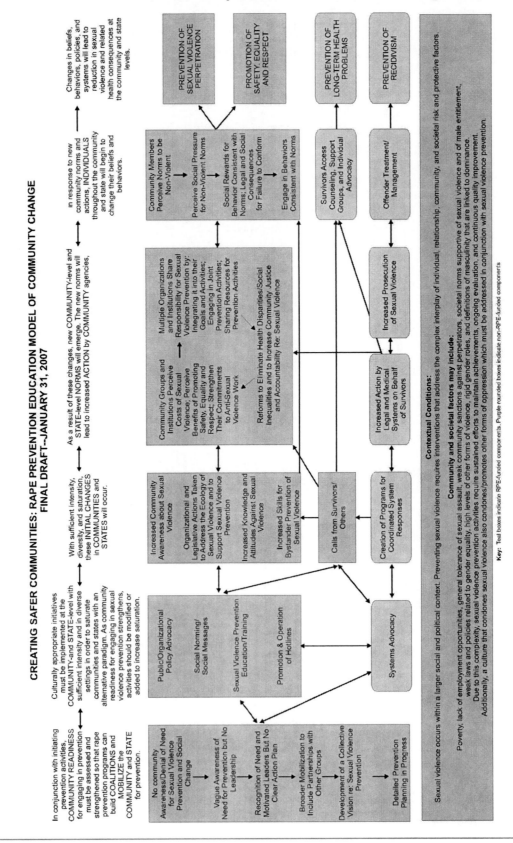

CREATING SAFER COMMUNITIES: RAPE PREVENTION EDUCATION MODEL OF COMMUNITY CHANGE
FINAL DRAFT—JANUARY 31, 2007

Exhibit 3

Exhibit 3 (Chapter 3) Kellogg Foundation Logic Model Development Guide Templates
How to use a Logic Model Through the Life of Your Program

CLARIFYING PROGRAM THEORY:

1. **PROBLEM OR ISSUE STATEMENT:** Describe the problem(s) your program is attempting to solve or the issues(s) your program will address.

2. **COMMUNITY NEEDS/ASSETS:** Specify the needs and/or assets of your community that led your organization to design a program that addresses the problem.

3. **DESIRED RESULTS (OUTPUTS, OUTCOMES AND IMPACTS):** Identify desired results, or vision of the future, by describing what you expect to achieve near- and long-term.

4. **INFLUENTIAL FACTORS:** List the factors you believe will influence change in your community.

5. **STRATEGIES:** List general successful strategies or "best practices" that have helped communities like yours achieve the kinds of results your program promises.

6. **ASSUMPTIONS:** State the assumptions behind *how* and *why* the change strategies will work in your community.

DEMONSTRATING YOUR PROGRAM'S PROGRESS:

1. **OUTPUTS:** For each program activity, identify what outputs (service delivery/implementation targets) you aim to produce.

2. **OUTCOMES:** Identify the short-term and long-term outcomes you expect to achieve for each activity.

3. **IMPACT:** Describe the impact you anticipate in your community in 7 to 10 years with each activity as a result of your program.

4. **ACTIVITIES:** Describe each of the activities you plan to conduct in your program.

5. **RESOURCES:** Describe the resources or influential factors available to support your program activities.

PROGRAM EVALUATION QUESTIONS AND INDICATORS:

1. **FOCUS AREA:** From your program theory logic model, list the components of the most important aspects of your program.

2. **AUDIENCE:** Identify the key audiences for each focus area. Who has an interest in your program?

3. **QUESTIONS:** For each focus area and audience, list the questions they may have about your program.

4. **INFORMATION USE:** For each audience and question you have identified, identify the ways you will use the evaluation information.

5. **INDICATORS:** Describe what information could be collected that would indicate the status of your program and its participants for each question.

6. **TECHNICAL ASSISTANCE:** Indicate the extent to which your organization has the evaluation and data management expertise to collect and analyze the data that relates to this indicator.

Exhibit 3a (Chapter 3)
Kellogg Foundation Program Implementation Template
This document is available as a PDF or in MS WORD through www.wkkf.org. Search "resources and evaluation"
(Note the time-frame is different below as short-term for programs is defined as 1-3 years, compared to this guide referring to initial victim outcomes as minutes, hours, or days)

Logic Model Development

Program Implementation Template

RESOURCES	ACTIVITIES	OUTPUTS	SHORT- & LONG-TERM OUTCOMES	IMPACT
In order to accomplish our set of activities we will need the following:	*In order to address our problem or asset we will accomplish the following activities:*	*We expect that once accomplished these activities will produce the following evidence or service delivery:*	*We expect that if accom-plished these activities will lead to the following changes in 1-3 then 4-6 years:*	*We expect that if accom-plished these activities will lead to the following changes in 7-10 years:*

Exhibit 3b(Chapter 3)
Kellogg Foundation Program Planning Template
This document is available as a PDF or in MS WORD through www.wkkf.org. Search "resources and evaluation"

Logic Model Development
Program Planning Template

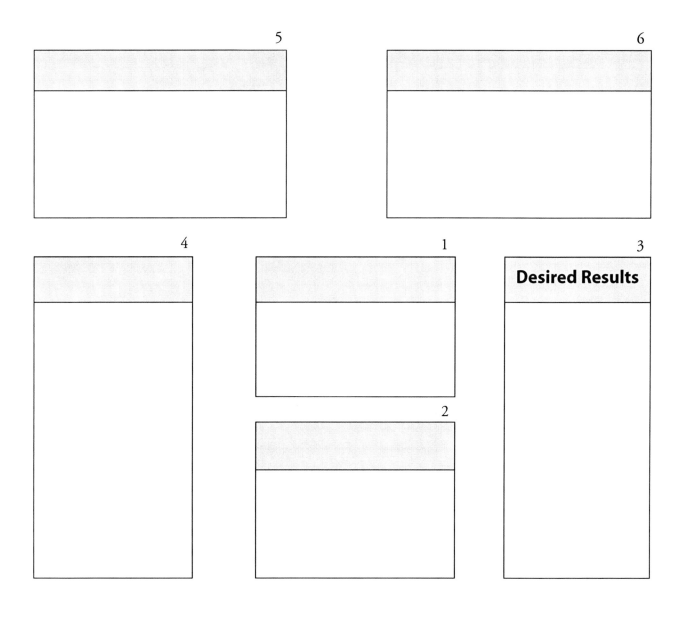

Exhibit 3c (Chapter 3)
Kellogg Foundation Evaluation Planning Template
This document is available as a PDF or in MS WORD through www.wkkf.org. Search "resources and evaluation"

Logic Model Development

Evaluation Planning Template

Evaluation Focus Area	Audience	Question	Use

Exhibit 3d (Chapter 3)
Kellogg Foundation Indicators Development Template
This document is available as a PDF or in MS WORD through www.wkkf.org. Search "resources and evaluation"

Logic Model Development

Indicators Development Template

Focus Area	Question	Indicators	Technical Assistance Needed

Exhibit 4a
Safety Outcome Model with sample activities for each outcome

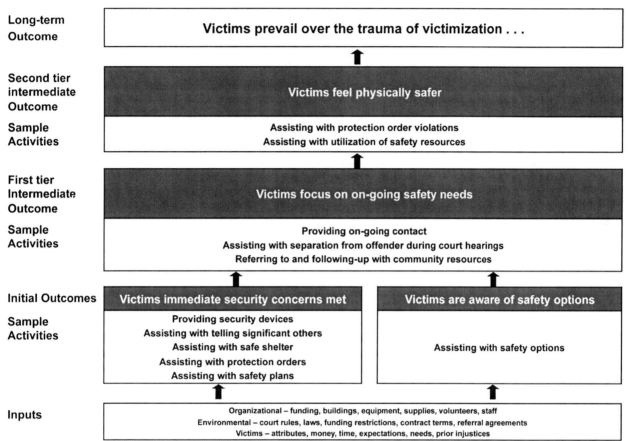

Crime Victim Services' Outcome Model for SAFETY

Long-term Outcome
> Victims prevail over the trauma of victimization . . .

Second tier intermediate Outcome
> Victims feel physically safer

Sample Activities
> Assisting with protection order violations
> Assisting with utilization of safety resources

First tier Intermediate Outcome
> Victims focus on on-going safety needs

Sample Activities
> Providing on-going contact
> Assisting with separation from offender during court hearings
> Referring to and following-up with community resources

Initial Outcomes
> Victims immediate security concerns met
> Victims are aware of safety options

Sample Activities
> Providing security devices
> Assisting with telling significant others
> Assisting with safe shelter
> Assisting with protection orders
> Assisting with safety plans

> Assisting with safety options

Inputs
> Organizational – funding, buildings, equipment, supplies, volunteers, staff
> Environmental – court rules, laws, funding restrictions, contract terms, referral agreements
> Victims – attributes, money, time, expectations, needs, prior injustices

NOTE: For each activity listed above, the number of outputs are the number of activities provided to victims.

Exhibit 4b
Healing Outcome Model with sample activities for outcomes

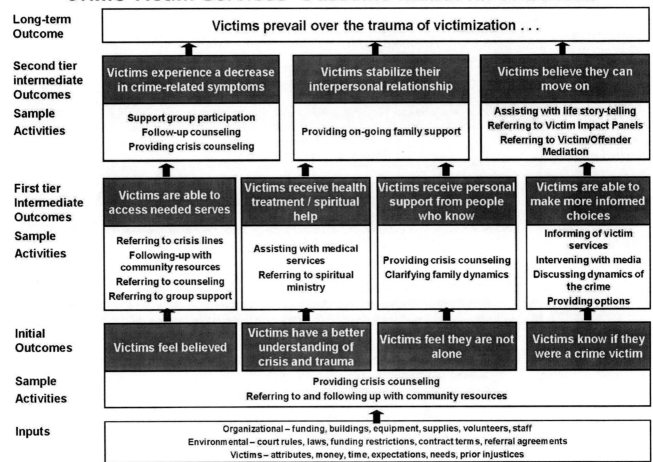

Crime Victim Services' Outcome Model for HEALING

Long-term Outcome

Victims prevail over the trauma of victimization . . .

Second tier intermediate Outcomes

| Victims experience a decrease in crime-related symptoms | Victims stabilize their interpersonal relationship | Victims believe they can move on |

Sample Activities

| Support group participation Follow-up counseling Providing crisis counseling | Providing on-going family support | Assisting with life story-telling Referring to Victim Impact Panels Referring to Victim/Offender Mediation |

First tier Intermediate Outcomes

| Victims are able to access needed serves | Victims receive health treatment / spiritual help | Victims receive personal support from people who know | Victims are able to make more informed choices |

Sample Activities

| Referring to crisis lines Following-up with community resources Referring to counseling Referring to group support | Assisting with medical services Referring to spiritual ministry | Providing crisis counseling Clarifying family dynamics | Informing of victim services Intervening with media Discussing dynamics of the crime Providing options |

Initial Outcomes

| Victims feel believed | Victims have a better understanding of crisis and trauma | Victims feel they are not alone | Victims know if they were a crime victim |

Sample Activities

Providing crisis counseling
Referring to and following up with community resources

Inputs

Organizational – funding, buildings, equipment, supplies, volunteers, staff
Environmental – court rules, laws, funding restrictions, contract terms, referral agreements
Victims – attributes, money, time, expectations, needs, prior injustices

NOTE: For each activity listed above, the number of outputs are the number of activities provided to victims.

Exhibit 4c
Justice Outcome Model with sample activities for each outcome

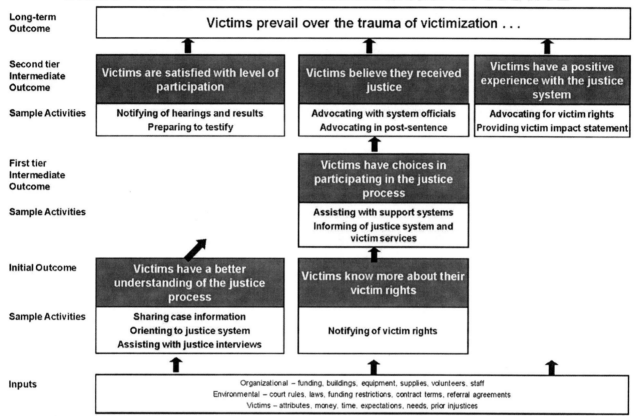

Crime Victim Services' Outcome Model for JUSTICE

Long-term Outcome	Victims prevail over the trauma of victimization . . .		
Second tier Intermediate Outcome	Victims are satisfied with level of participation	Victims believe they received justice	Victims have a positive experience with the justice system
Sample Activities	Notifying of hearings and results / Preparing to testify	Advocating with system officials / Advocating in post-sentence	Advocating for victim rights / Providing victim impact statement
First tier Intermediate Outcome		Victims have choices in participating in the justice process	
Sample Activities		Assisting with support systems / Informing of justice system and victim services	
Initial Outcome	Victims have a better understanding of the justice process	Victims know more about their victim rights	
Sample Activities	Sharing case information / Orienting to justice system / Assisting with justice interviews	Notifying of victim rights	
Inputs	Organizational – funding, buildings, equipment, supplies, volunteers, staff / Environmental – court rules, laws, funding restrictions, contract terms, referral agreements / Victims – attributes, money, time, expectations, needs, prior injustices		

NOTE: For each activity listed above, the number of outputs are the number of activities provided to victims.

Exhibit 4d
Restitution Outcome Model with sample activities for each outcome

Crime Victim Services' Outcome Model for RESTITUTION

Long-term Outcome	Victims prevail over the trauma of victimization . . .
Second tier Intermediate Outcome	Victims recover financially
Sample Activities	Assisting with community and family resources Documenting Compensation paid to victim Documenting restitution paid to victim
First tier Intermediate Outcome	Victims on-going financial needs met
Sample Activities	Submitting and documenting court restitution orders Assisting with filing Victims Compensation Attaching bond for restitution
Initial Outcomes	Victims know about Victim Compensation for violent crime / Victims' emergency financial needs are met
Sample Activities	Providing Victims Compensation information / Providing emergency financial options and assistance
Inputs	Organizational – funding, buildings, equipment, supplies, volunteers, staff Environmental – court rules, laws, funding restrictions, contract terms, referral agreements Victims – attributes, money, time, expectations, needs, prior injustices

NOTE: For each activity listed above, the number of outputs are the number of activities provided to victims .

Exhibit 4e
Victim Ministry Outcome Model

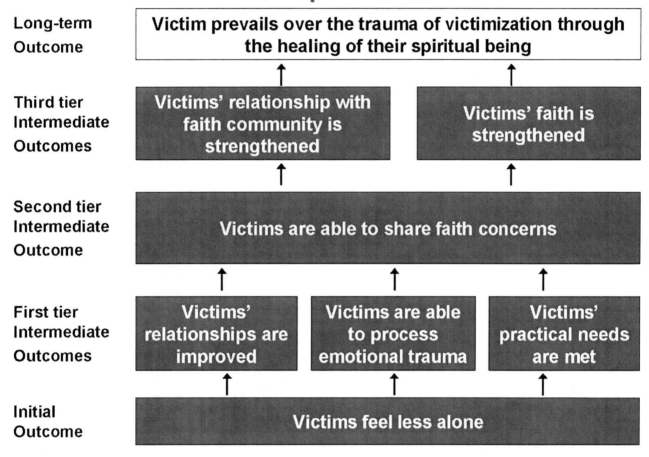

Exhibit 4f
Victim Impact Panel Outcome Model

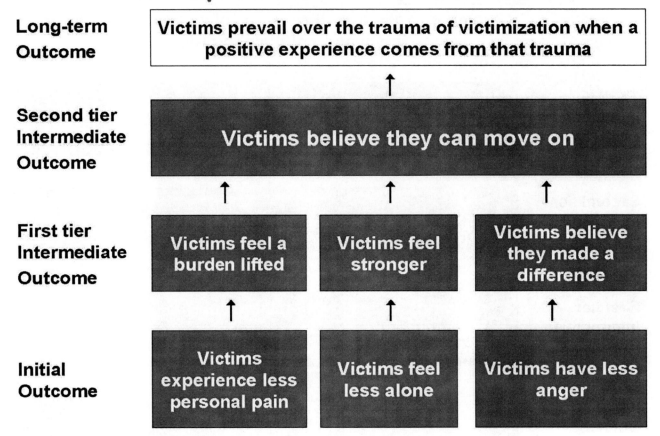

Victim Impact Panel Outcome Model

Long-term Outcome	Victims prevail over the trauma of victimization when a positive experience comes from that trauma
Second tier Intermediate Outcome	Victims believe they can move on
First tier Intermediate Outcome	Victims feel a burden lifted / Victims feel stronger / Victims believe they made a difference
Initial Outcome	Victims experience less personal pain / Victims feel less alone / Victims have less anger

Exhibit 4g
Domestic Violence Support Group Outcome Mode

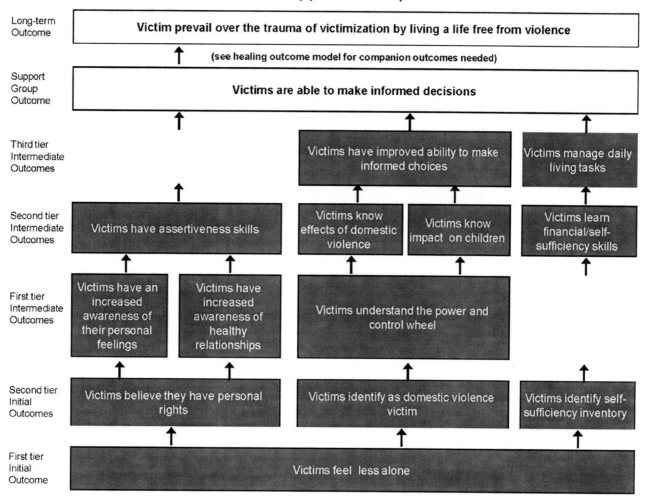

Exhibit 4h
Victim Outcome Model for Victim Offender Dialogue (Mediation)
with sample activities for each outcome

VICTIM Outcome Model Victim Offender Mediation

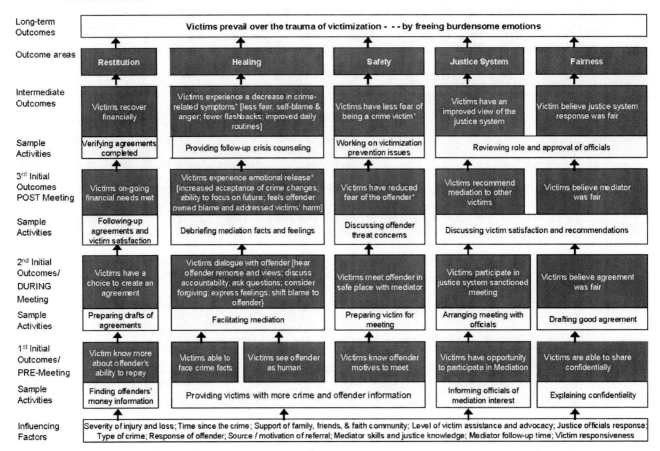

	Restitution	Healing	Safety	Justice System	Fairness
Long-term Outcomes	Victims prevail over the trauma of victimization - - - by freeing burdensome emotions				
Outcome areas	Restitution	Healing	Safety	Justice System	Fairness
Intermediate Outcomes	Victims recover financially	Victims experience a decrease in crime-related symptoms* [less fear, self-blame & anger; fewer flashbacks; improved daily routines]	Victims have less fear of being a crime victim*	Victims have an improved view of the justice system	Victim believe justice system response was fair
Sample Activities	Verifying agreements completed	Providing follow-up crisis counseling	Working on victimization prevention issues	Reviewing role and approval of officials	
3rd Initial Outcomes POST Meeting	Victims on-going financial needs met	Victims experience emotional release* [increased acceptance of crime changes; ability to focus on future; feels offender owned blame and addressed victims' harm]	Victims have reduced fear of the offender*	Victims recommend mediation to other victims	Victims believe mediator was fair
Sample Activities	Following-up agreements and victim satisfaction	Debriefing mediation facts and feelings	Discussing offender threat concerns	Discussing victim satisfaction and recommendations	
2nd Initial Outcomes/ DURING Meeting	Victims have a choice to create an agreement	Victims dialogue with offender [hear offender remorse and views; discuss accountability; ask questions; consider forgiving; express feelings; shift blame to offender]	Victims meet offender in safe place with mediator	Victims participate in justice system sanctioned meeting	Victims believe agreement was fair
Sample Activities	Preparing drafts of agreements	Facilitating mediation	Preparing victim for meeting	Arranging meeting with officials	Drafting good agreement
1st Initial Outcomes/ PRE-Meeting	Victim know more about offender's ability to repay	Victims able to face crime facts / Victims see offender as human	Victims know offender motives to meet	Victims have opportunity to participate in Mediation	Victims are able to share confidentially
Sample Activities	Finding offenders' money information	Providing victims with more crime and offender information		Informing officials of mediation interest	Explaining confidentiality
Influencing Factors	Severity of injury and loss; Time since the crime; Support of family, friends, & faith community; Level of victim assistance and advocacy; Justice officials response; Type of crime; Response of offender; Source / motivation of referral; Mediator skills and justice knowledge; Mediator follow-up time; Victim responsiveness				

Note: Increased knowledge of offender and case facts can reduce feeling of safety and healing recovery

Exhibit 4i
Offender Outcome Model for Victim Offender Dialogue (Mediation)

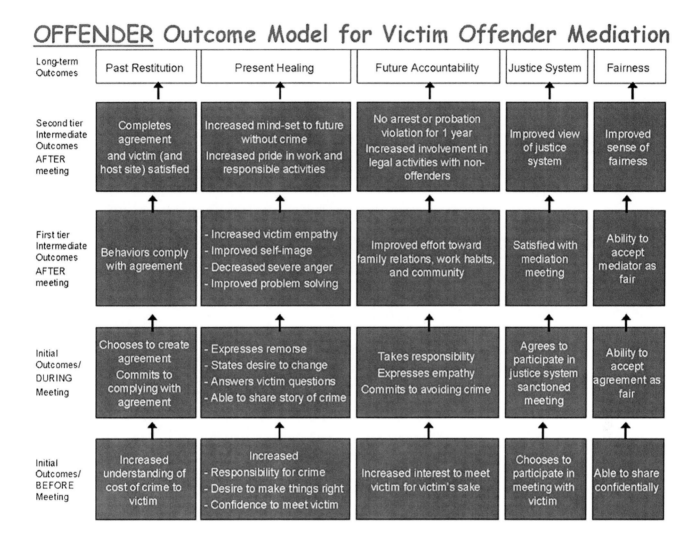

OFFENDER Outcome Model for Victim Offender Mediation

	Past Restitution	Present Healing	Future Accountability	Justice System	Fairness
Long-term Outcomes	Past Restitution	Present Healing	Future Accountability	Justice System	Fairness
Second tier Intermediate Outcomes AFTER meeting	Completes agreement and victim (and host site) satisfied	Increased mind-set to future without crime; Increased pride in work and responsible activities	No arrest or probation violation for 1 year; Increased involvement in legal activities with non-offenders	Improved view of justice system	Improved sense of fairness
First tier Intermediate Outcomes AFTER meeting	Behaviors comply with agreement	- Increased victim empathy; - Improved self-image; - Decreased severe anger; - Improved problem solving	Improved effort toward family relations, work habits, and community	Satisfied with mediation meeting	Ability to accept mediator as fair
Initial Outcomes/ DURING Meeting	Chooses to create agreement; Commits to complying with agreement	- Expresses remorse; - States desire to change; - Answers victim questions; - Able to share story of crime	Takes responsibility; Expresses empathy; Commits to avoiding crime	Agrees to participate in justice system sanctioned meeting	Ability to accept agreement as fair
Initial Outcomes/ BEFORE Meeting	Increased understanding of cost of crime to victim	Increased - Responsibility for crime; - Desire to make things right; - Confidence to meet victim	Increased interest to meet victim for victim's sake	Chooses to participate in meeting with victim	Able to share confidentially

Exhibit 5

Exhibit 5 (Chapter 5)
Sample Victim Survey Summary

Each survey item is related to a quality area (access, structure, process, and outcome) and an outcome area (safety, healing, justice, and restitution/financial recovery). One satisfaction item is last, and is separated from the rest since some victims choose to complete only one item before returning the survey.

The business/organization survey is shortened (items 1,2, 3, 9, 10, 12, 13, and 14) for property crimes (e.g. theft, vandalism, fraud, bad checks). The outcome area of restitution/financial recovery is lacking since business are not eligible for victim compensation. Some ideas to substitute: "I am more aware of financial recovery options through this program" (an initial outcome) and "I have begun (or expect) to receive some repayment due to the assistance of this program" (an intermediate outcome).

The quality areas and indicators include:

1. Access—I was able to contact this program when I needed to

2. Process—I was treated with respect by program staff

3. Structure—The services I needed were available at, or through, this program

4. Initial Outcome: safety—This program has helped make me more aware of my safety options

5. Intermediate Outcome: safety—I feel physically safer because of the help I received through this program

6. Initial Outcome: healing—I feel less alone since working with this program

7. Initial Outcome: healing—I have a better understanding of my crisis and trauma

8. Intermediate Outcome: healing—I believe that I can move on past the trauma effects of this crime

9. Initial Outcome: justice—I know more about my legal rights since working with this program

10. Initial Outcome: justice—I have a better understanding of how the justice process works

11. Initial Outcome: restitution—I know about Ohio's Victim Compensation Fund for victims of violent crime since working with this program

12. Process—My phone calls to this program were returned within 48 hours

13. Process—I received court hearing notices on time from this program

14. Satisfaction—I am satisfied with the services I received from this program

The length of time question explores any correlation with initial and intermediate outcomes, type of crimes, and other survey items or demographics. Reverse questions were not selected as they caused too much victim confusion. For example, a negative statement (e.g. I did NOT have phone calls returned promptly) requires a positive experience response to switch to *disagree*. Demographic questions complete the survey.

Exhibit 5a
Sample Victim Survey

Crime Victim Services Program Survey

Please help us improve and inform funders of our services

SKIP any statement that does not apply to you	Strongly Agree	Agree	Neutral	Disagree	Strongly Disagree
I was able to contact this program when I needed to	5	4	3	2	1
I was treated with respect by program staff	5	4	3	2	1
The services I needed were available at, or through, this program	5	4	3	2	1
This program has helped make me more aware of my safety options	5	4	3	2	1
I feel physically safer because of the help I received through this program	5	4	3	2	1
I feel less alone since working with this program	5	4	3	2	1
I have a better understanding of my crisis and trauma	5	4	3	2	1
I believe that I can move on past the trauma effects of this crime	5	4	3	2	1
I know more about my legal rights since working with this program	5	4	3	2	1
I have a better understanding of how the justice process works	5	4	3	2	1
I know about Ohio's Victim Compensation Fund for victims of violent crime since working with this program	5	4	3	2	1
I know how to register for victim notification (VINE) since working with this program	5	4	3	2	1
My phone calls to this program were returned within 48 hours	5	4	3	2	1
I received court hearing notices on time from this program	5	4	3	2	1

	Strongly Agree	Agree	Neutral	Disagree	Strongly Disagree
I am satisfied with the services I received from this program	5	4	3	2	1

How long ago did this crime occur? _____ less than 2 months   _____ 2-6 months   _____ more than 6 months

Please help us with data about yourself or the victim if you are answering for him / her

Age: ___ 0-12   Ethnicity: ____ African-American   Gender: ____ Male
       ___ 13-17   ____ Asian   ____ Female
       ___ 18-29   ____ Caucasian
       ___ 30-44   ____ Hispanic
       ___ 45-64   ____ Native-American
       ___ over 65   ____ Other

Is English your first language?   ___ Yes   ___ No

Please feel free to comment about Crime Victim Services staff or services on the back of this sheet. Thank you.

Please feel free to contact us.

Allen County   **Putnam County**
419-222-8666   **419-523-1111**
Web site: www.CrimeVictimServices.org
E-mail: victim@CrimeVictimServices.org

United Way | United Way of Greater Lima & Putnam County

Office Use:		
Type of Crime:	❏ Violence/Stalking /	Received:
❏ Homicide / Murder	Home Burglary/Robbery	❏ Mail
❏ Sexual Assault	❏ Property/Theft/	❏ In Person
❏ Domestic Violence	Bad Checks/ Child Support	❏ Telephone

G:\WPDOCS\Outcome Measurement\Surveys\Survey Revisions 09-17-08.wpd

Exhibit 5b (Chapter 5)
Sample Survey for Business or Organization

Crime Victim Services Program Survey
For Your Business or Organization

Please help us improve and inform funders of our services

SKIP any statement that does not apply to you	Strongly Agree	Agree	Neutral	Disagree	Strongly Disagree
I was able to contact this program when I needed to	5	4	3	2	1
I was treated with respect by program staff	5	4	3	2	1
The services I needed were available at, or through, this program	5	4	3	2	1
I know more about my legal rights since working with this program	5	4	3	2	1
I have a better understanding of how the justice process works	5	4	3	2	1
I know how to register for victim notification (VINE) since working with this program	5	4	3	2	1
My phone calls to this program were returned within 48 hours	5	4	3	2	1
I received court hearing notices on time from this program	5	4	3	2	1

I am satisfied with the services I received from this program	5	4	3	2	1

How long ago did this crime occur? ____less than 2 months   ____2-6 months   ____more than 6 months

Please feel free to comment about Crime Victim Services staff or services below or on the back of this sheet. Thank you.

Please feel free to contact us.

Allen County	**Putnam County**
Crime Victim Services	**Crime Victim Services**
116 W. North Street	**338 E. Third Street**
Lima, OH 45801	**Ottawa, Ohio 45875**
419-222-8666	**419-523-1111**

Web site: www.CrimeVictimServices.org
E-mail: victim@CrimeVictimServices.org

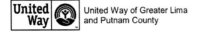 United Way of Greater Lima and Putnam County

G:\WPDOCS\Outcome Measurement\Surveys\Business Survey 10-01-07.wpd

Exhibit 6

Exhibit 6 (and Exhibit 7 following) (Chapter 6)
Executive Director Job Description
(expanded version)

Mission Statement: To help victims prevail over the trauma of their victimization by assisting & advocating for safety, healing, justice, and restitution

Position Description: To implement the Mission of Crime Victim Services. The major strategies are to assure *access* to services, to provide needed services within a sustainable organizational *structure*, to assure a sensitive *process* of services, and to attain *outcomes* that improve victim's lives. Goals are to be attained with a collaborative spirit and integrity, recognizing that the service quality, reputation, financial solvency, and efficiency of the organization are delegated to the executive director. Responsibilities include leadership excellence in the following areas:

Access—victims know about, can find, and are able to utilize services that are:

1. **Visible** - Provide public awareness and positive reputation of services

   a) Publicize services with public service announcements (e.g. radio, T.V., and billboards)

   b) Display posters and brochures in public areas; assure 24 hour visible signage, etc.

   c) Work with media for event coverage, submit editorials and articles, offer interviews, etc.

   d) Do public speaking across jurisdiction in places of worship, clubs, associations, etc.

   e) Maintain 24 hour web site with service information, links, and program contacts

   f) Publish newsletter conveying expertise, availability, and victim outcomes

2. **Accessible**—Provide services reachable by full population

   a) Enhance parking, facility, and proximity with partners to benefit victims

   b) Assure handicap accessible entrance, bathroom, services, and phone contacts

   c) Maintain 24 hour domestic violence and rape crisis line

   d) Assure access for limited-English speakers, particularly for Spanish language

   e) Assure seamless transition from first contact to receiving services

3. **Acceptable**—Assure welcoming and safe initial contacts

   a) Enhance and maintain inviting internal area of facility (e.g. entrance and waiting area)

   b) Maintain cared-for exterior appearance (e.g. sidewalk, weeds, trash, flowers, and snow)

   c) Assure warm voice tone and non-verbal greetings in initial contacts

d) Maintain safe and confidential contacts and environment

4. **Available**—Assure services are available for prompt use

a) Maintain service availability (e.g. shelter beds, appointments, and case information)

b) Assure phone, office, and e-mail have prompt response during scheduled hours

c) Assure updated collaboration agreements, referral processes, and partner cross training

Structure—provide right services, right staff, and right organization, including:

1. **Governance**—Create and maintain excellent design and operation of organization

a) Administer budget, financials, fundraising, and reporting with accuracy and transparency

b) Complete income searching, applying, implementing, relationship building and reporting

c) Protect and grow reserves and endowment funds

d) Assure clean audit, proper insurance, and check & balance systems (mail, petty cash)

e) Assist with board agendas, recruitment and recognition, and committees

f) Assure proper data management for victims, statistics, outcomes, and grants

2. **Partnerships**—Create and maintain seamless victim advocacy across organizations

a) Assure cross-communication with law enforcement, prosecutor, probation and court

b) Promote collaborations enhancing quantity, quality, access and process victim advocacy

i) Task forces for rape crisis, domestic violence, children, elderly, mental and developmental disabled

ii) Collaboration with hospital emergency rooms, billing, and Forensic Nurse Examiners

iii) Collaboration with Legal Aid, interpreters, and counselors

iv) Collaboration with Family Justice Center, and social service and United Way network

c) Maintain volunteer, intern, places of worship, and community involvement opportunities

d) Manage protocols to assure victim advocacy predictability and cross-communication

3. **Tools**—Design and maintain excellent, efficient, and effective internal functionality

a) Assure equipment, software, and work areas are updated and adequate

b) Protect confidentiality and safety of victims

c) Assure updated and user-friendly agency and victim materials and displays

d) Provide accurate, efficient, and secure data management system

e) Assure victim and program evaluation process with at least 10% responding

Exhibit 6

4. **Staff**—Assure that staff are competent, productive, safe, and victim-outcome focused

a) Update, implement, and enforce (in a positive manner) agency and personnel manuals

b) Prioritize national and state advocate credentialing and service standards

c) Assure focus on victim-outcomes with resources, routine guidance and evaluations

d) Promote culture of praise, ongoing learning, mutual support and work place enjoyment

e) Assure regular training for job duties, diversity, ethics, outcomes and vicarious trauma

f) Prioritize pay and benefits, participatory leadership, and low turnover rate

5. **Services**—Design, provide, and adapt victim-driven services

a) Provide leadership for needs assessment and strategic planning every 5-7 years

b) Assure services are specific for variety of victim needs and linked to outcomes

c) Assure services are specific for victims at different levels of participation and need

d) Promote collaborations enhancing quantity, quality, access, and process of advocacy

i) For felony, misdemeanor, juvenile, and post-conviction victim needs

ii) For unreported, unsolved, complex, cross-jurisdictional, and restorative justice needs

e) Assure needs are addressed for emergency money and on-going spiritual needs

f) Provide special outreach services for disabled, at-risk, and re-victimization prevention

Process—respectful and personalized treatment of victims, including conduct that is:

1. **Ethical**—Maintain integrity and openness

a) Assure compliance with National Victim Assistance Ethical Standards

b) Promote full range of victim participation and service choices

c) Assure victims have desired and adequate support needs met to receive services

d) Assure victim feedback is welcome, including evaluation, grievance, and privacy options

2. **Professional**—Maintain high standards of appearance and work product

a) Assure accurate and timely notices and information

b) Literature wording understandable and readable for all populations

c) Dress code and non-verbal cues reflect crime seriousness, compassion, and respect

d) Victim prepared for hearings & involved in processes

3. **Unique**—Maintain individualized advocacy

a) Promote respect of victim faith issues and appropriate spiritual support services

b) Assure acceptance of each victims' interests, biases and fears

c) Prioritize respect, understanding, and response for each victim story and needs

d) Assure cultural and trauma sensitivity in word, deed, and service environments

e) Prioritize victim personal and legal rights and fair treatment

f) Prioritize victim driven treatment plan and victim selection of services

4. Sensitive—Maintain victim-centered advocacy

a) Prioritize vertical victim advocacy from time of crime until victim exit or recovery

b) Assure timely, prompt, on-task and reliable advocacy and response

c) Prioritize actual and perceived victim security needs

d) Provide options for restorative justice thinking and healing

e) Promote open-ended and friendly case closing for future victim re-contacts

f) Promote recognition of anniversary date of violence—as appropriate

g) Educate justice officials, legislators, and public policy officials regarding victim issues

Outcomes—improving victims' lives:

1. Promote Safety—E.g., Shelter, Protection Orders, emergency phones, new locks

2. Promote Healing—E.g. Crisis counseling, family support, medical issues, support group

3. Promote Justice—E.g. Court advocacy, timely and accurate hearing notices, witness help

4. Promote Restitution—E.g. state compensation, offender payment, emergency money

Efficient and Positive Leadership—serves with integrity, including:

1. Assuring efficient use of resources

2. Maintaining high standards of quality and ethics in services and management

3. Providing positive and mission focused leadership with a vision for the future

Exhibit 6

Executive Director Job Description
(short version)

Mission Statement: To help victims prevail over the trauma of their victimization by assisting and advocating for safety, healing, justice, and restitution

Position Description: To implement the mission of Crime Victim Services. The major strategies are to assure *access* to services, to provide needed services within a sustainable organizational *structure*, to assure a sensitive *process* of services, and to attain *outcomes* that improve victim's lives. Goals are to be attained with a collaborative spirit and integrity, recognizing that the service quality, reputation, financial solvency, and efficiency of the organization are delegated to the executive director. Responsibilities include leadership excellence in the following areas:

A) Access—victims know about, can find, and are able to utilize services that are:

1. Visible—Provide public awareness and positive reputation of services
2. Accessible—Provide services reachable by full population
3. Acceptable—Assure welcoming and safe initial contacts
4. Available—Assure services are available for prompt use

B) Structure—provide right services, right staff and right organization, including:

1. Governance—Create and maintain excellent design and operation of organization
2. Partnerships—Create and maintain seamless victim advocacy across organizations
3. Tools—Design and maintain excellent, efficient, and effective internal functionality
4. Staff—Assure that staff are competent, productive, safe, and victim-outcome focused
5. Services—Design, provide, and adapt victim-driven services

C) Process—respectful and personalized treatment of victims, including conduct that is:

1. Ethical—Maintain integrity and openness
2. Professional—Maintain high standards of appearance and work product
3. Unique—Maintain individualized and victim-centered advocacy
4. Sensitive—Maintain friendly and empathetic victim contacts

D) Outcomes—improving victims' lives with:

1. Safety—actual and perceived
2. Healing—spiritual, emotional, and medical
3. Justice—fairness and system treatment
4. Restitution—emergency resources and financial stability

E) Efficiency and Positive Leadership—serves with integrity, including:

1. Efficient use of resources
2. High standards of quality and ethics in services and management
3. Positive and mission focused leadership with a vision for the future

Exhibit 6

Executive Director Performance Management Form
(Chapter 6)

Director name: Evaluation date ___/___/___	Board members on Evaluation Committee:
Last evaluation date ___/___/__	Director start date __ /___/__ Board evaluation approval date___/___/___

Reason for Evaluation:

___Annual   ___End of probation   ___Unsatisfactory performance   other:_____

Definition of Performance Ratings:

5 - **Outstanding.** Performance is exceptional in all areas.

4 - **Very Good.** Results clearly exceed position requirements. Performance is high quality and consistent.

3 - **Good.** Competent and dependable level of performance. Meets performance standards of the job.

2 - **Improvement Needed.** Performance is deficient in certain areas. Improvement is necessary.

1 - **Unsatisfactory.** Results are generally unacceptable and require immediate improvement.

Performance Categories

1. Access to services: _____total

    A. _____ Visible—Providing public awareness and positive reputation
    B. _____ Accessible—Providing services reachable by full population
    C. _____ Acceptable—Assuring welcoming and safe initial contacts
    D. _____ Available—Assuring services are available for prompt use

Comments and Goals:

2. Structure of services and organization: _____total

    A. _____ Governance—Creating and maintaining excellent design and operation of organization
    B. _____ Partnerships—Creating and maintaining seamless victim advocacy across organizations
    C. _____ Tools—Design and maintaining excellent, efficient, and effective internal functionality
    D. _____ Staff—Assuring staff that are competent, productive, safe, and victim-outcome focused
    E. _____ Services—Designing, providing, and adapting victim-driven services

Comments and Goals:

3. Process of treating victims: _____total

    A. _____Ethical—Maintaining accountability for ethical standards, conflicts of interest and confidentiality
    B. _____Professional—Maintaining high standards for staff appearance, conduct and work product
    C. _____Unique—Maintaining victim-centered and individualized cultural and language advocacy
    D. _____Sensitive—Maintaining customer friendly advocacy

Comments and Goals:

4. Effort toward outcome of services in changing lives: _____total

    A. _____Promoting Safety—actual and perceived
    B. _____Promoting Healing—spiritual, emotional, and medical
    C. _____Promoting Justice - fairness and system treatment
    D. _____Promoting Restitution/financial stability—emergency, compensation, and in-kind resources

Comments and Goals:

5. Efficiency and Positive Leadership: _____total

    A. _____Assuring efficient use of resources
    B. _____Maintaining high standards of organization, documentation, reporting, and supervision
    C. _____Providing positive mission focused leadership and a vision for the future

Comments and Goals:

Executive Director Comments and Goals:

Final Rating:

Total score from all categories = _____

Comment Sheet Attached   _____ Yes   _____ No

Executive Director signatureand date   Board President signature and date

Exhibit 7

Exhibit 7 (Chapter 6)
Sample Activity Manual Table of Contents
with sample activities to help attain each outcome

SAFETY - Initial Outcomes

#1 Victims immediate security concerns met

---

1. Assessment Issues
   a) Ask, "Are you safe?"
   b) Contact information
   c) Description of situation and persons involved
   d) Law enforcement involvement
   e) Telling significant others
2. Security Devices
   a) 911 phones
   b) Personal alarms
   c) Video and audio recording options
   d) New or changed locks
   e) Pre-paid phones and phone cards
3. Protection Orders
   a) Review eligibility criteria
   b) Civil and criminal options
   c) Time-frame and enforcement issues
   d) Conditions to offender bond & probation
   e) Divorce and child custody restraints & orders
4. Safety Assessment
   a) Lethality matrix
   b) Abuse index
5. Safety Plan
   a) Education information
   b) Personalized plan
   c) Local and internet options
   d) On-line security issues
   e) Journaling and documentation
6. Safe Shelter
   a) Family and friends
   b) Safe homes & neighbors
   c) Hotel and motel
   d) Domestic violence and rape crisis shelter
   e) Homeless shelter
   f) Pet care and farm animal care
7. Transportation
   a) Access to vehicle and fuel
   b) Options for taxi, bus, train, etc.
   c) Community services and places of worship
   d) Staff and volunteers

#2 Victims are aware of safety options

1. Explore particular fears
2. List individual safety options
3. Prioritize needs
4. Preview access and costs
5. Discuss alternatives
6. Provide referrals
7. Follow-up as needed

SAFETY—First Tier Intermediate Outcome #3 Victims focus on ongoing safety needs

1. Discuss safety situation
   a) Ask victim to describe fears
   b) Do not minimize fears
   c) Assess positive actions taken
   d) Discuss support system
   e) Review prior incidents and what happened
   f) Discuss possible future violations by offender
   g) Review priority and realism of fears
2. Safety Assistance
   a) Review and revise safety plan
   b) Protection Order violations
   c) Victim separation from offender at court, home, and work
   d) Safety anxiety and stress symptoms
   e) Transitional and permanent housing
   f) Relocation Assistance
   g) Electronic surveillance (detection and installation)
   h) Reporting procedure and jurisdiction if needed
3. Referrals
   a) Discuss desire for offender custody notification
   b) Internet sites for checking offender status
   c) Need for victim home security checks
   d) Provide contact information for referrals

SAFETY Second Tier Intermediate Outcome #4 Victims feel physically safe

1. Safety Assistance
   a) Review safety plan
   b) Review safety devices
   c) Review offender release, release conditions and notification
2. Offender expungement eligibility
3. Victimization Prevention
   a) Review safety environment—emotional and physical
   b) Safe family and friends who will help
   c) Discuss most feared and likely victimization
   d) Review safety plan options
   e) Promote realism and positive attitude

Exhibit 7

HEALING - Initial Outcomes
5 Victims know if they were a victim

1. Crisis counseling
   a) Listen to story
   b) Talk about gut feelings
   c) Review facts and witnesses
   d) Discuss violation feeling
   e) Note evidence and memory may not last
2. Referrals
   a) Possible law enforcement and prosecutor help
   b) Self-help materials and web sites
   c) Medical testing and other verification ideas

#6 Victims feel less alone

1. Crisis Counseling
   a) Say "I'm glad you called"
   b) Discuss confidentiality
   c) Offer help with or without arrest
   d) Reassure they are not crazy
   e) Consider other support people
   f) Assure that venting feelings is okay
   g) Encourage telling story and feelings
   h) Note availability and openness to talk
2. Share Time and Thoughts
   a) Meet and eat together
   b) Send "Thinking of you" cards
   c) Find family and friends commonalities
   d) Make and accept check-up phone calls
   e) Note personal and identifying info for future
3. Referrals
   a) Offer chance to talk with other victims
   b) Note support group options
   c) Explore spiritual issues and referrals
   d) Discuss co-worker, friends, others
   e) Offer meeting victims on Victim Impact Panels
   f) Ask if interested in mental health counseling
4. Crisis Lines
   a) Domestic violence
   b) Sexual assault
   c) Mental health crisis lines & web sites
   d) National hotlines for different victims

#7 Victims feel believed

1. Crisis Counseling
   a) Say, "I'm sorry).."
   b) Rephrase what's heard
   c) Ask, "Are you feeling...?"
   d) Do you have other support people?
   e) Who have you told?
   f) Have you reported it to law enforcement?
   g) Positive reinforcement
2. Create Action Plan
   a) Gather information
   b) Discuss options - filing charges, law enforcement, family, hospital
   c) What to expect next
   d) Self-help ideas—material and web sites
   e) Contact information and plan
   f) Review and agree on plan
3. Implement Plan
   a) Review possible poor response of officials
   b) Keep communicating

#8 Victims have a better understanding of their crisis & trauma

1. Crisis Counseling
   a) Identify common feelings
   b) Loss of control
   c) Feeling violated
   d) Grieving loss, trust, and injury
   e) Anger is normal
   f) Stress of extra work
   g) Life routine disrupted
   h) Perspective of seriousness
   i) Hassle and problem of crime
   j) Medical and physical issues
   k) Specifics of victimization impact & reactions
   l) Invitation to call back

Exhibit 7

HEALING—First Tier Intermediate Outcomes
#9 Victims receive health treatment and spiritual help

1. Review medical needs & health treatment
   a) Legal and cost issues
   b) Follow-up testing or treatment
   c) Medical supplies
   d) Transportation
   e) Hospital and clinic options
   f) Department of Health
   g) Emergent Care
   h) Dental
   i) Prescriptions
   j) Medical supplies
   k) Home health
2. Spiritual side of safety, hope, trust, & peace
   a) Explore faith relationships and beliefs
   b) Ask about supportive faith persons
   c) Discuss faith strengths, options, and priorities
3. Referral options & contacts
4. Eliminate Barriers
   a) Identify from to-do list
   b) Gently review options for resolution
   c) How can I help?
   d) Make plan and assignments
   e) Follow-up on referral tasks for victim to-do
   f) More non-blaming follow-up

#10 Victims receive personal support from people who know

1. Assess & develop support
   a) Who knows?
   b) Who do you want to know?
   c) Who can you tell?
   d) Reminder—once told, a genie is out of the bottle
2. Crisis Counseling
   a) Discuss current trusting relationships
   b) Review family members who are close
3. Help with support people
   a) Material and videos
   b) Suggest using articles to share hard things
   c) Offer home visit to help tell support people
   d) Library and Internet resources for support team
   e) Clarify what victims want people to know now

11 Victims are able to make more informed choices

1. Crisis Counseling areas
   a) Strengths and weaknesses
   b) Positive empowerment
   c) Change process
   d) Current default and desired personality
   e) Family dynamics and impact on decisions
2. Areas of Choices
   a) Media involvement
   b) Justice process
   c) Learning about healing
   d) Counseling and specialty areas

#12 Victims are able to access needed services

    1. Identify possible service needs
    2. Discuss priority of needs
    3. Link specific needs with service options
    4. Find provider services information
a) Contact
b) Location
c) Coverage area
d) Cost
e) Transportation
f) Availability of services (waiting lists)
g) Verify information with provider
    1. Review choices and priorities
b) Assist with task list
c) Discuss priorities
d) Support small steps to accomplishing tasks
e) Discuss barriers and tasks to overcome
f) Review Victim Advocate support and follow-up

Exhibit 7

HEALING—Second Tier Intermediate Outcomes
13 Victims experience a decrease in crime-related symptoms

1. Extreme Anger
   a) Discuss how anger feels
   b) Encourage non-destructive anger
   c) Discuss how anger affects them
   d) Accept anger without judgment
   e) Do not minimize anger (do not try to talk them out of it)
   f) Validate right to be angry
   g) Do not ask "why" questions
2. Unable to do Routine Tasks
   a) Discuss changes in routine
   b) Encourage buddy system
   c) Encourage task segmentation
   d) Identify and validate small successes
   e) Encourage positive self-talk
   f) Identify areas of control & validate
3. Nightmares & Flashbacks
   a) Encourage relaxation techniques
   b) Discuss bedtime patterns
   c) Encourage physical exam
   d) Note impacts of drugs and alcohol use
4. Self Blame
   a) Discuss self blame directly
   b) Do not ask "why" questions
   c) Reassure offender responsibility
5. Isolation & Loneliness
   a) Listen and explore feelings
   b) Explore support options

14 Victims stabilize interpersonal relationships

1. Provide Acceptance and Caring
   a) Odd reactions are normal and not crazy
2. Note People Express Differently
3. Self Value and Awareness
4. Priority of Current Needs
5. Family and Friend Dynamics
6. Healthy Talk and Routines
7. Wish List and To Do List
8. Anticipate Reactions of Others
9. Taking Action
10. Adapting and New Support Relationships

#15 Victims believe they can move on

1. Ask About Life Changes
    a) Since first knowledge, reactions and support need
2. Help Summarize Story and Big Picture context
3. Discuss Who Is or Is Not Providing Support
4. Reality of Life, Job, and People
5. What is Important in Life
6. What Can and Can't Change
7. Vision for Direction and New Reality in Life
8. Action Plan and First Steps

JUSTICE - Initial Outcomes #16 Victims have a better understanding of the justice process

1. Explain Entry Point Process
    a) School, hospital, law enforcement, child or adult protective services
    b) Crime scene issues & system responses
    c) Options of law enforcement reporting
    d) Process of arrest, warrant, summons, etc.
    e) Public information, media, and privacy rights
2. Investigation Process
    a) Police report
    b) Victim gathering and providing information
    c) Detective role (if assigned)
    d) Early charges may not reflect full crime
    e) Prosecutors role in level and timing of charges
3. Justice System Process
    a) Initial appearance and arraignment
    b) Written not guilty pleas
    c) Bond conditions and victim information needed
    d) Victim protection and stay away conditions
    e) Bond violation reporting and process
4. Explain Juvenile, Misdemeanor or Felony
    a) Victim rights and options various stages
    b) Interviews, evidence collection, and offender rights
5. Pleas Bargain/Motion Hearings
6. Pre-Sentence Investigation
7. Sentencing and Disposition
8. Probation, Jail, and Prison (flat and open-ended time)
9. Local & State Notification Systems

Exhibit 7

#17 Victims know more about victim rights

1. Inform of Victim Rights
2. Provide Rights and Contact Information
    a) informed, present, heard, restitution and safety
    b) Offer time and help to understand
    c) State brochures and legal information
    d) Web sites and knowledgeable sources
    e) Case update and notification letters

JUSTICE—First Tier Intermediate Outcome #18 Victims have choices in the justice process

1. Police Reporting Options
2. Prosecution Options
    a) Written or verbal Victim Impact Statement
    b) Court attendance and speaking vs. subpoena
    c) Sentencing recommendations and restitution
3. Post-Sentencing—notices, reviews, etc.

JUSTICE—Second Tier Intermediate Outcomes #19 Victims are satisfied with level of participation

1. Intervention Options
    a) Interview with law enforcement/investigator
    b) Walk through and understand proceedings
    c) Meet with prosecutor
    d) Victim recommend protocol changes
    e) Role of media
    f) Victim writing and telling story
    g) Participate in Victim Impact Panel
    h) Participate in Victim Offender Mediation
    i) Write letter to officials or media
    j) Voice concerns with privacy, hearing dates, etc.
2. Discuss Case Specifics
    a) System options (e.g. no ex-parte with judge)
    b) Legal advice from prosecutor or private lawyer
    c) Perceived disincentives or disrespect
    d) Impact of participation
    e) Support people perceptions
    f) Ask if victim believed, heard and supported

#20 Victims believe they received justice

1. Discuss Case Specifics
   a) Note similar case result averages
2. Early and Current Victim Feelings of Justice
   a) When feelings changed
   b) How did it make you feel?
3. Complaint and Appeal Options
   a) Bar association and attorney disciplinary office
   b) Media story and Letter to Editor
   c) Office director and elected official
   d) Write as an example
   e) Victim rights compliance options
   f) Compliment or complaint to state association
   g) Protest options, e.g. picket, petitions, and march
   h) Volunteer for system and victim programs
4. Civil Justice Options
5. Review Sentencing and Conditions
6. Discuss Non-System Justice and Results
7. Note Appeals, Notices, Expungement, etc.

#21 Victims have a positive experience with the justice system

1. Treatment by Officials
   a) Law Enforcement
   b) Prosecutors
   c) Judges and court personnel
   d) Victim Advocates
   e) Probation/Parole
   f) Clerk of Courts
   g) Victim rights protected
   h) Express appreciation for sharing and participating

RESTITUTION - Initial Outcomes
#22 Victims know about Victim Compensation

1. Review Eligibility for State Victim Compensation
2. Provide Information and Application
3. Review Time Frames and Procedures
4. Encourage and Assist with Application
5. Offer Future Support and Information
6. Follow-up with Victim Regarding Filing

Exhibit 7

#23 Victims emergency financial needs are met

1. Emergency Fund
   a) Reimburse victim
   b) Advance pay to victim
   c) Arrange payment by phone to provider
   d) Credit card
   e) Letter to provider to delay, use payment plan, or guarantee payment
2. Referrals
   a) Salvation Army
   b) Red Cross
   c) Thrift Store
   d) Food pantry
   e) Federal Emergency Management Agency (FEMA emergency funds)
   f) State assistance options

RESTITUTION—First Tier Intermediate Outcome
#24 Victims on-going financial needs are met

1. Follow-up for Victims Compensation from State
   a) Eligibility and time frames for filing
   b) Filing process and assistance
   c) All bills filed
   d) Need and options for expedited process
   e) Appeal process
   f) Confirm payment received (or provide intervention advocacy)
2. Restitution from Criminal
   a) Payment update
   b) Prosecutor filing motions to prompt paying
   c) Probation and parole enforcement options
   d) Attach bond money
   e) Pay victim before criminal pays court costs
   f) Proper notices to custody or rehabilitation site
3. Insurance
   a) Home owners for property
   b) Medical & dental for health
   c) Property owner and civil suit options

RESTITUTION—Second Tier Intermediate Outcome #25 Victims recovery financially
1. Review Overall Financial Impact of Crime 2. Ask about any Special Problems 3. Discuss Recovery Process and Participants 4. Acknowledge Violation and Successes 5. Offer Future Assistance as Needed 6. Ask about Ideas for Personal Improvement 7. Ask Who Deserves Appreciation for Progress

Exhibit 7a (Chapter 6)
Sample Activity Manual Illustration

for outcome # 13—Victims experience a decrease in crime-related symptoms. In other words, if you opened the activity manual for help with addressing outcome # 13, you might find these traumatic emotions cheat sheets (a short and a longer version).

Traumatic emotions SHORT VERSION—1.5 pages (for posting near desk or phone)

EXTREME ANGER: Anger is a form of energy and must be released and managed effectively. Anger is a common emotion to most people, but victims of crime often feel that extreme anger is taking control of their lives.
*   Encourage venting anger in nondestructive ways.
*   Ask how the anger feels (physical and emotional sensations).
*   Ask how the anger is affecting them and their lives.
*   Accept angry words without judgment.
*   Do not minimize the anger or attempt to talk the victim out of what they feel.
*   Validate their right to be angry.
*   Do not ask "why" questions as they may induce thoughts of self-blame.
*   Reinforce that anger is a normal reaction to victimization.

UNABLE TO DO ROUTINE TASKS: Victims often feel unable to go about their lives as they did prior to the crime. A crisis state may render the victim incapacitated. Support from a Victim Advocate may be critical.
*   Discuss observable changes in daily routine or ask the victim to identify changes noted.
*   Encourage the victim to create a buddy system. Finding support may facilitate focus.
*   Encourage task segmentation.
*   Ask to identify and validate small successes, e.g. making a call to the Victim Advocate.
*   Introduce and encourage positive self-talk.

FEAR FOR PERSONAL SAFETY: Fear can be a crippling and overpowering emotion. Victims may experience an increased sense of vulnerability to real or perceived dangers. Assess for weapons or potential lethality.
*   Ask victims to describe and express fears.
*   Do not minimize fears.
*   Help assess positive actions to enhance safety.
*   Assist in defining support system.

NIGHTMARES/FLASHBACKS: A common reaction to victimization, this response can be highly unsettling and frightening. The victim may be irritable, nervous and exhausted.
*   Encourage learning relaxation techniques.
*   Assist in examining bedtime patterns.
*   Encourage a medical physical discourage use of drugs or alcohol unless medically directed.
*

SELF BLAME: Victims often look back on their trauma and assign themselves responsibility in some way. It is important that the victim be reassured that they hold no fault in their victimization.
*   Listen for self-blame and confront it directly. "I hear you blaming yourself for . . . "
*   Do not ask "why" questions.
*   Reassure the victim that they are not to blame for another's violent behavior.

<u>ISOLATION/LONELINESS:</u> Victims may feel that their victimization sets them apart from the rest of the community. Shame, guilt, and fear may be factors contributing to loneliness and isolation.
- Listen for indications of loneliness and introduce into the conversation. "You sound . . . "
- Explore support options and assist linkage. Assist with first crucial step if necessary.
- Reinforce Victim Advocates' support role.

<u>FEELING OUT OF CONTROL:</u> Victims often feel their lives are spiraling out of control and believe that regaining control is out of their reach.
- Listen for and identify indicators of loss of control.
- Assist in noting where control is maintained and validate these successes.
- Encourage positive self-talk.
- Assist in establishing support systems.
- Encourage learning relaxation techniques.

<u>Activities Manual # 13 traumatic emotions</u> LONGER VERSION—3 ½ pages

<u>In General:</u>
Do Not Say:
"I know how you feel." (every situation is different)
"Don't cry, it'll be okay." (crying is a healthy release of emotion and should be encouraged)
"You'll get over it." (no one ever fully gets over victimization)
"At least..." or, "You're lucky that..." (there was nothing lucky about being a victim)
"It's God's will..." or, "God only gives us what we can handle..." (maycause victim to be angry at God when support is needed)
Do Say:
" I'm sorry this happened to you."
"It's harder than most people realize."
"What you are going through is very hard and you're doing a great job."
"It wasn't your fault."
"I believe you."
"It is okay to feel_____."
"I am here to listen..." or "Are you able to tell me about what happened?"
"What can I do to assist you?"

<u>1. Extreme Anger</u>
Anger is a form of energy that needs to be released and managed effectively. Although a common emotion to most people, victims of crime often feel their anger is taking control of their lives. Encourage victims to vent their anger or frustration in non-destructive but energy releasing ways such as shredding paper, screaming to the top of their lungs, hitting a pillow, or using words (any of their choice) to voice anger. Victim Advocates can encourage the venting of anger by asking the victim to describe how the anger feels including both physical and emotional sensations. Avoid using "why" questions as they can appear to assign blame. A victim experiencing extreme anger should be referred for professional counseling. Assess the appropriate time to inquire about participation on the Victim Impact Panel, Victim Offender Mediation, or Victim Ministry.
Do Not Say:
1. "Don't be angry."
2. "Calm down" or "relax."
3. "Why did you...?"
4. "You'll get over it."

5. "Time heals all wounds."
6. "It is God's will."
Do Say:
1. "Tell me about your anger" or "What's the worst part of being so angry?"
2. "It is normal reaction to feel angry."
3. "Call me if you want to, or come in and talk."
4. "You are safe to vent with me. Our conversations are confidential."
5. "Who can you can talk to when you are feeling angry?"

2. Unable To Do Routine Tasks

The Victim Advocate should take note of observable changes in the daily routine of the victim. The victim can also be asked to identify changes in their daily routine. These observations can be used as an entry point fordiscussion. Encourage the victim to find someone to assist them with tasks. The creation of a buddy system can facilitate motivation and focus. The victim may find it useful to start with task segmentation. By dividing the task into small parts and undertaking them one at a time the victim may ultimately be able to move beyond paralysis and restore independence. This is also an opportunity for the Victim Advocate to introduce or reinforce the concept of positive self-talk. Subsequent contacts with the victim should be used to strengthen this simple but effective technique.

Professional counseling may be indicated. A victim exhibiting a high degree of distress may initially need some additional support as a crisis state may render them virtually incapacitated. They may benefit from the strength and encouragement from the Victim Advocate. Assist with setting up the initial appointment with the therapist and offer to go along if victims desires. This extra support may aid the victim in taking the first crucial step toward healing. Assess for dependency over time and talk about it with the victim if necessary.
Do Not Say:
1. "It's easy."
2. "Just try harder."
3. "You can do anything you put your mind to."
Do Say:
1. "What you are feeling is a common reaction."
2. "It is okay to feel distracted or out of control."
3. "Who can share these tasks with you?"
4. "Describe a task you are able to accomplish." (Consider simple tasks such as calling the Victim Advocate.)

3. Fear for persons safety:

Fear can be a crippling and overpowering emotion. It may be useful to assist the victim in differentiating between fear and anxiety. Encourage the victim to express their fears andanxieties and look for concrete solutions. Acknowledge that fear is a normal reaction and the victim should accept this emotion without feeling guilty or foolish. Ask about guns or other weapons—the availability to both the victim and offender. Use the information to assess lethality and act accordingly, including assisting the victim in looking at the reality and consequences of weapons. Help the victim identify healthy and safe choices. Victims may experience an increased sense of vulnerability to other perceived dangers as well. Do not diminish these fears—they are real to the victim. Discuss ways to take positive action and enhance safety (alarms, police safety checks, window or door blocks, answering machine and/or caller ID).
Do Not Say:
1. "It won't happen again."
2. "God won't give you more than you can handle."
3. "Try to forget it, think about something else, just get over it." or "It's time to move on."
Do Say:
1. "Let's discuss ways to enhance your safety."

2. "What you are feeling is a normal reaction."
3. "Tell me about your fears."

4. Nightmares or flashbacks:

This is a common reaction to victimization and can be highly unsettling and frightening. It may seem to the victim that there is no escape from the trauma of the crime. The victim may become irritable and exhausted. Learning relaxation techniques may help reduce the after effects of the nightmare or enhance other restful periods. Encourage healthy habits such as nutrition, exercise, and stress reducing practices. Discuss bedtime patterns for routines potentially disruptive to sleep. Possibly discuss avoidance of alcohol and drugs, getting a physical, and the option of mental health and counseling.

Do Not Say:
1. "Don't let it bother you so much, it's over."
2. "I know how you feel."
3. "That dream must mean..."

Do Say:
1. "This is a common response of victims."
2. "Who can you talk to about your pain?".
3. "I am here and I care about you."
4. "I'm sorry."
5. "What can I do to assist you?"

5. Self Blame:

Victims often look back at their trauma and assign themselves responsibility in some way. They may blame themselves and feel guilty that a personal action (or inaction) may have placed themselves or others at undo risk. It is important to reassure the victim that they hold no fault in theirvictimization. Counseling and/or an appropriate support group may prove beneficial. Assess for Victim Offender Mediation, Victim Ministry, or Victim Impact Panel.

Do Not Say:
1. "Why were...?" or "Why was...?" (Why questions may appear to assign blame)
2. "If I had been in your situation" or, "You should have..."
3. "Don't feel that way."

Do Say:
1. "You are not to blame."
2. "You are not the cause of another person's violent behavior."
3. "Tell me your story."
4. "Who can you count on for support?"

6. Isolation/Loneliness:

Victims may feel that the trauma of their crime sets them apart from the rest of the community. Shame, fear and guilt may be factors contributing to loneliness and isolation. Life changes that result from the crime may feel insurmountable. Explore support systems available to the victim and help them connect if necessary. Refer to the appropriate support group that may serve as a vital first step.

Do Not Say:
1. "Just get back out there."
2. "You will feel better soon."

Do Say:
1. "You are not alone. You were very brave to ask for help."
2. "With whom can you share your pain?"
3. "I am here and I care about what you have been through."

4. "I will check back with you from time to time." (And do it.)

7. Feeling Out Of Control:

Victims often feel they have lost control over many areas of their lives as a result of the victimization. They may feel finding a way to take back control is out of their reach, a lesson often taught to victims of domestic violence by their batterer. The Victim Advocate may assist the victim by helping them to identify and validate small steps taken toward gaining control. Overcompensation sometimes manifestsin angry, highly controlling behavior. In this case, the Victim Advocate should not respond to the anger, but may need to set appropriate limits. The victim should be assessed for participation on Victim Impact Panels, Victim Offender Mediation, or Victim Ministry. Refer to the appropriate support group and counseling.

Do Not Say:

1. "Relax" or "Calm down."
2. "Be thankful that..."
3. "I know how you feel. "

Do Say:

1. "I am here to listen."
2. "You've taken a big step in contacting me."
3. "I will check back if it is okay with you." (And do it.)
4. "What can I do to assist you?

Exhibit 8

Exhibit 8 (Chapter 6)

Logic Model for Writing and Evaluating Grants (a non-profit business plan)

			sample domestic violence (DV) grant items
Condition / Problem Statement – 20 points			
		Score by the level to which the applicant ...	
The problem Why and to whom this problem matters, and evidence-based options for response	How do you know it is the problem? Has the problem and severity been researched & a local needs assessment been done?	1) Identifies & documents problem with statistics and distinguishes between the problem and its symptoms (5 pts) 2) Identifies target population (size & characteristics) and appropriateness of service (linkage between problem & population & service) (5 pts) 3) Provides data demonstrating short and long-term community impacts of the problem (5 pts) 4) Provides information about evidence-based solutions, including varying use of resources, collaborations, and significance of influencing factors (5 pts)	1) Data for national, state, & local DV deaths / trauma 2) Data re: DV deaths of women leaving abuse & specificity of local issues 3) Data for economic, social, and family costs / harm 4) Data for solution options; rank good options and their local influencing factors
Program Description – 20 points			
Why this program is the answer for this problem	Does the response link to the problem, and provide access and customer / site specific services?	5) Explains the evidence-based solution selected for the local program, including criteria used and local adaptations and influencing factors (5 pts) 6) Demonstrates that appropriate collaborations exist or are created, and explains collaboration rationale & goals (5 pts) 7) Demonstrates access to program is sufficient (5 pts) 8) Demonstrates process of assuring and measuring quality client treatment and smooth flow of services (5 pts)	5) Shelter reduces death and repeat DV; crisis line links safety, money, and support 6) Police + shelter, peer + family support, money +job 7) Awareness data & planning 8) Gender, geography, diversity, language issues
Inputs and Organizational Capacity – 10 points			
INPUTS Nouns What we invest and our limitations (e.g., laws)	What will it take to get the job done? What are the resources needed?	9) Identifies the local resources as correct for the response, including how the composition and history of the organization and collaboration link to likely success (5 pts) 10) Details staff levels, training, dedication, and experience to successfully implement the program and accomplish its goals (5 pts)	9) Agency & partners have agreements & history of DV safety, support & money 10) Staff awards, leadership and experience as a team for this cause & grant task
Activities and Timeline – 10 points			
ACTIVITIES Verbs What we do and how we do it	Are activities in order and proportional to the task and time allotted?	11) Provides clear strategies and actions for all the key elements and populations of the program description / implementation (5 pts) 12) Includes reasonable and incremental timeframes to accomplish activities, & explains phases of progress (5 pts)	11) List activities 24 / 7 for DV safety, support & financial 12) Describe activities linked by time, staff effort, & victim participation / role
Program Outputs and Objectives – 10 points			
OUTPUTS A Number Counting the work done in the right time	Does the work product match the activities and link to the description?	13) Details work product and progress from the activities, including baseline data showing results as ambitious yet reasonable and likely to result form the activities (5 pts) 14) Links and verifies the output results are correct and timely for the program description / implementation (5 pts)	13) E.g., # of sessions for safety planning (& plans) and staff hours per activities 14) E.g., Safety & support outputs linked to isolation
Program Outcomes and Measures – 25 points			
OUTCOMES The Change Making a difference in people's lives	What impact does the program have in people's lives? Is the model logical and monitored?	15) Documents the desired outcomes as evidence-based or promising practice, and reasonable for this program (5 pts) 16) Demonstrates that outcomes represent incremental progress in program induced changes in clients (5 pts) 17) Links outcomes with inputs, activities and outputs (5 pts) 18) Demonstrates that the outcomes (and quality levels) address the problem, target population, and community impact (5 pts) 19) Demonstrates outcome changes are measured & monitored for influencing factors, inputs, activities & outputs (5 pts)	15) Research linking DV issues & clinical / victim outcomes 16) Logic model of initial, inter-mediate, long-term outcomes 17) Use chart with arrows 18) Match death / injury problem with safety outcome 19) Note plan for reviewing and adapting whole process
Sustainability – 5 points			
Stability Staying power	Will the program remain?	20) Demonstrates that resources and collaborations are cultivated with communication, transparent reporting and good governance structure	20) Note agreements, reporting content and priorities, and review & governance plan
Efficiency – Bonus 5 points			
Cost per outcome	Is maximum value provided?	21) Demonstrates measures to monitor and adapt inputs, activities & outputs for maximum outcomes from investment	21) Compare cost analysis with similar programs

Exhibit 8a (Chapter 6)

Grant Logic Model "lite" – adapted for United Way funding

Condition / Problem Statement – 5 points (1 page) Score by the level to which the applicant (within page limit) …			sample rape crisis (RC) grant content
Explain the problem	How do you know it is the problem?	1) Identifies & documents the problem, with short and long-term impacts, using two sources with statistics and quotes, and distinguishes between the problem and its symptoms (5 pts)	1) Data for national and local sexual assault crime, trauma and economic effects, etc.
Program Description – 20 points (2 pages)			
How this program is the answer for this problem	What solutions does research suggest? Is it collaborative and provide customer friendly access and service?	2) Provides information about evidence-based solutions, and demonstrates the local response selected is appropriate to the problem, including linkage between problem, solution, population (size and characteristics), and program (5 pts) 3) Demonstrates that the appropriate collaborations exist or are created to address the key problem areas (5 pts) 4) Demonstrates access to program is sufficient (5 pts) 5) Demonstrates process of assuring and measuring quality client treatment and smooth flow of services (5 pts)	2) Research response options and criteria used for local crisis line, counseling, and on-call to hospital Emer Rm 3) Nurse, prosecutor, police, and shelter protocols in use 4) Detail publicity and "no wrong door" availability 5) Victim-friendly audit report
Inputs & Organizational Capacity- 10 pts (2 pages: input, activities & outputs)			
INPUTS Nouns What we invest and our limitations	Do you have what it takes to get the job done? Is the staff qualified?	6) Identifies how the structure, history, and resources of the organization link to likely success (5 pts) 7) Details staff levels, training, dedication, and experience to successfully implement the program and accomplish its goals (5 pts)	6) Cross-jurisdictional, single mission, & long agency history 7) Professional and personal commitment of staff to problem and local solution skills needed
Activities and Timeline – 10 points			
ACTIVITIES Verbs What we do and how we do it	Are activities correct and proportional to the task and time allotted?	8) Identifies strategies and services for the problem response selected, including an implementation and daily activity summary (5 pts) 9) Includes reasonable and incremental timeframes to accomplish activities, including phases of progress (5 pts)	8) Length and type of support group and counseling, protocol responses – phone, hospital… 9) On-going service. Media timed with summer, TV shows.
Program Outputs and Objectives – 5 points			
OUTPUTS A Number Counting work done	Does the work product match the activities?	10) Details work product and progress from the activities, including baseline data showing output targets as ambitious yet reasonable	10) Target numbers linked with prior years data, similar programs, support groups and crisis line usage, etc.
Program Outcomes and Measures – 20 points (logic model + 2 pages)			
OUTCOMES The Change Making a difference in people's lives	Are lives changed? Are the logic model parts connected? Are measures and outcomes monitored?	11) Documents the desired outcomes as evidence-based or promising practice, and reasonable for this program (5 pts) 12) Demonstrates that outcomes represent incremental progress in program induced changes in clients (5 pts) 13) Links outcomes with inputs, activities and outputs (5 pts) 14) Demonstrates that indicators and outcome process is monitored and adapted. Note communication and governance structure for cultivating partners (5 pts)	11) Studies show early trauma needs are local outcomes 12) Submit outcome logic model 13) Explain examples of links in logic model between parts 14) Bi-annual review half-days for results and changes, with elected leaders
Sustainability – 10 points (1 page)			
Staying Power	Is program stable?	15) Rates financial sustainability structure of funds (5 pts) 16) Links outcomes with key financial expenses (5 pts)	15) Rate top 10 funds security 16) Personnel links to outcomes
United Way Collaboration – 20 points (3 checklists + ½ page)			
Team Effort	What role did you play in this partnership?	17) Demonstrates prior year collaboration with itemization of: a) community publicity (5 pts), b) campaign involvement (5 pts), c) committee participation (5 pts) 18) Responds to prior year recommendations (5 pts)	17) Complete list of United Way publicity and involvements 18) Specify what changes were made to problems noted

Acknowledgments

Special thanks go to the grantors that helped fund the development of these ideas, however, none of the views represented in this book necessarily reflect their views: a grant from the United Way of Greater Lima Endowment Fund (Lima, Ohio) which helped develop and integrate outcomes into the fabric of the organization; a grant from the United States Department of Justice Office for Victims of Crime Training and Technical Assistance Center, Washington, D.C., which helped develop the outcome model; a grant from the United States National Institute of Corrections Technical Assistance, Washington, D.C., which helped develop the Victim and Offender outcome models for Mediation; and a grant from the Bluffton University Research Center, Bluffton, Ohio, which helped redesign the victim survey tool and evaluate the outcome measure data.

On a more personal note, I would also like to give special thanks to three groups of people. First are the many crime victims who are now my friends and from whom I have learned. Then there are the experts who extensively edited and advised on the manuscrip: Lois Wetherill (President of Crime Victim Services Board of Directors), Joan Zorza (Editor of the Domestic Violence Report and the Sexual Assault Report), Jeannette Adkins (former Executive Director of the National Organization for Victim Assistance), J. Douglas Bailey (President of Performance Vistas), and David S. Adams, Ph.D. (retired Sociology professor and outcome trainer). Finally, I must mention and thank the many supporters who helped me: Jodi Warnecke, former Assistant Director, Crime Victim Services; Susan Howley, Public Policy Director, National Center for Victims of Crime; Karla Stephens and Ernest Hutchins, Ohio Attorney General's Office; Steve Derene, Executive Director, National Assoc. of VOCA Victim Assistance Administrators; Anne Seymour, Editor of The Crime Victims Report; Michael Hendricks, United Way of America outcome author and consultant; Leland and Joanne Voth, my parents; Luke and Cindy Voth, my son and his wife; Eva Voth, my daughter; and Laura Voth, my wife and best friend.

LaVergne, TN USA
17 February 2010
173386LV00001B/198/P